WATCHING THE BOTTOM LINE

WATCHING THE

HOW TO MASTER THE ESSENTIAL TECHNIQUES FOR MANAGING SMALL BUSINESSES FINANCES

BOTTOM LINE

Profitability is the key to your business survival

JOHN WHITELEY

howtobooks

First published in 2004 by
How To Books Ltd, 3 Newtec Place,
Magdalen Road, Oxford OX4 1RE. United Kingdom.
Tel: (01865) 793806. Fax: (01865) 248780.
email: info@howtobooks.co.uk
http://www.howtobooks.co.uk

British Library Cataloguing in Publication Data
A catalogue record for this book is available from the British
Library

Cover design by Baseline Arts Ltd, Oxford
Produced for How To Books by Deer Park Productions,
Tavistock, Devon
Typeset by PDQ Typesetting, Newcastle-under-Lyme, Staffs.
Printed and bound by Cromwell Press, Trowbridge, Wiltshire

NOTE: The material contained in this book is set out in good
faith for general guidance and no liability can be accepted
for loss or expense incurred as a result of relying in particular
circumstances on statements made in the book. The laws and
regulations are complex and liable to change, and readers should
check the current position with the relevant authorities before
making personal arrangements.

Contents

Introduction

TAKING CONTROL

Small businesses often find more difficulty than large businesses in managing their resources, and finance is one of the most important resources. The key to management of any resource is the ability to take control of it. Throughout this book, you will find important key ideas. Here is the first, which will be repeated in several different contexts: if you can't measure it, you can't control it.

The key to financial control is accurate measurement. In order to measure things accurately, certain techniques must be learnt. Those techniques form the bulk of this book.

THE ART AND CRAFT OF FINANCIAL MANAGEMENT

This subject is not simply a matter of learning techniques. Certain personal attitudes of mind and interpersonal skills must be cultivated. Of course these come with experience, but it is worth pointing out some of the basic elements, of which the first is: take nothing for granted – question everything.

For example, in cost accounting, you must understand the nature of each individual cost element. A costing system is a model of the business as a whole.

Retaining integrity

You must instil confidence in those with whom you deal. A bank manager will certainly be assessing the person as much as the business. Different groups – shareholders, customers, suppliers, employees, lenders and board members – will have different expectations which must be balanced against one another. Understanding and balancing these expectations calls for real interpersonal skills.

Profitability is the key to business survival – without it there will be no business to continue. But the moral and ethical dimension to managing finance must also be cultivated. Honesty and integrity must come before financial gain – either personally or for the business.

Keep the long-term interest of the business constantly in view.

Short-term decisions often conflict with the long-term prospects of the business. Businesses also have a wider responsibility to the environment, to society, and to the local community. If you can manage all these aspects you will earn the respect of others who matter and build up a reserve of goodwill – a most important asset.

Good communication should never deteriorate into 'spin' or manipulation of the facts and figures. Too many financial scandals and frauds have been the result of deliberate misrepresentation of figures so that they are misleading. In recent history, the names Enron and

Worldcom should be enough to remind everyone that the ultimate goal of communicating financial information is to present the situation as it really is.

Personal relationships

Managing finance involves cooperation with shareholders, with other people in the business, with customers and suppliers, and with bank managers or other lenders.

This book also touches on various non-financial areas of management. This is not accidental or a mistake. Understanding people in other areas is vital.

Developing communication skills

Learn the skills of communication, which means ensuring that the listener or reader understands the same message that you wish to convey.

You will have to communicate with:

◆ other managers;
◆ other employees;
◆ directors; and
◆ the public.

This requires the ability to express yourself clearly in written or spoken English, as far as possible without jargon. In finance matters particularly, and especially when dealing with board members or other managers, your audience may be embarrassed to ask for an explanation of something not understood. They may think that they should understand it, and be embarrassed about their lack of understanding.

Here is a golden rule of communication: never underestimate the intelligence of your audience, but never overestimate their knowledge of your specialist subject. More than that, learn to distinguish the relevant from the irrelevant, the material from the immaterial, the core from the peripheral. Oscar Wilde said that facts are 'seldom pure and never simple'. Facts – especially financial ones – usually need interpretation. The skilful financial manager will be able to offer meaningful comment on the implications of the choices put before the audience – whether that audience be the board of directors, other managers or shareholders.

Timeliness is essential in controlling the business and as the basis for decision-making. Many financial disasters could have been avoided if those responsible had communicated their financial information promptly. Directors and shareholders depend on financial managers to spot potential problems and crises before they materialise.

I have written this book assuming no prior knowledge of the subject, and have tried to avoid jargon and to explain concepts simply. There is a glossary of key terms at the end of the book and a list of websites that I trust will be helpful. I hope that you enjoy reading this book and that it proves useful.

Understanding Accounts

WHAT IS BEHIND THE FIGURES?

Business accounts are not just a jumble of figures on paper without any context; they are a representation of the reality of the business. A casual reader may look at financial statements, go straight to the bottom line to see what the profit is and leave it at that. Another might look at the turnover figures to see how the sales are going. Many people do not get further than a cursory glance because they do not understand the relationships between the various figures in the financial statements. Financial managers must see behind the figures, and learn to use comparisons, ratios and statistical analysis.

> Figures in accounts are not just numbers on a piece of paper. They represent something substantive – what is happening in the real world. Discovering what they mean is a vital tool in exercising control.

Types of accounts

External financial statements are issued once or twice a year for the benefit of shareholders or proprietors and lodged with Companies House. Company accounts can be subject to audit, depending on the size of the company, and they may not appear promptly after the end of the year.

In contrast, internal financial statements, generally known as management accounts, could be produced quarterly, monthly or even weekly. They are produced for the benefit of managers and should be produced extremely promptly.

Components of accounts

Any financial statements consist of a profit and loss account and/or a balance sheet. These forms may be expanded or adapted to suit the purpose for which they are prepared but essentially they are variations of the same thing.

A typical set of accounts, in abbreviated form, is shown in Figure 2.1, consisting of a profit and loss account and a balance sheet. The comparative figures for the immediately preceding period are shown on the right-hand side of the current figures.

Profit and loss account

This account is always for a stated period – usually, but not always, a year.

Income

The gross income, also known as turnover, consists of the core income from sales of products or services or whatever form the core income is. Other income from incidental sources is shown separately.

Direct costs

The direct costs (cost of sales) are deducted from the gross income to show the gross profit. The gross profit is a key

Profit and loss account for the year ended 31 December 20xx

	Current year		Previous year	
	£000	£000	£000	£000
Sales		500		450
Cost of sales		300		250
Gross profit		200		200
Other income		5		2
		205		202
Overheads		110		104
Net profit		95		98
Taxation	30		30	
Dividends	40		35	
		70		65
Retained profit		25		33

Balance sheet as at 31 December 20xx

Fixed assets		400		350
Current assets	130		114	
Current liabilities	65		59	
Working capital		65		55
		465		405
Long-term liabilities				
Loans		80		85
Net assets		385		320
Capital				
Share capital		150		120
Share premium		10		
Profit and loss account		225		200
Shareholders' funds		385		320

Figure 2.1. Specimen company accounts for the year ended
31 December 20xx

figure in the accounts, and its relationship to turnover is a key business indicator.

Overhead expenses
Overhead expenses are categorised into different types of expense, such as administration, property, transport, finance, etc. Understanding them gives an insight into how the business runs. The overhead expenses are deducted from the gross profit to arrive at the net profit or net loss. The relationship of net profit to turnover is another key business indicator.

Appropriations
Appropriations such as dividends and taxation of profit are deducted from the net profit (or loss).

The final figure after appropriations is retained profit (or accumulated losses).

In summary, the profit and loss account shows the result of the business activities for the period.

Balance sheet
The balance sheet is always given as at a particular date, which is always the final date of the period for which the profit and loss account is prepared.

The balance sheet shows the financial position of the business as at the date shown. The gross assets are shown, from which liabilities are deducted, leaving the net assets of the business.

Capital
In a limited company, the capital includes the share capital, and there may also be a share premium account (representing monies paid by shareholders in excess of the nominal value of the shares). The other element of capital is the accumulated reserves of the profit and loss account. There could also be other capital reserves, which are sometimes created when assets are revalued, and similar transactions.

In an unincorporated business, such as a partnership or a sole trader, the capital consists of the money put into the business by the proprietors, added to their shares of profits, and from which any monies drawn out of the business are deducted.

Whatever the form of the business, the capital will always be equal to the net assets of the business.

Another way of looking at the correspondence between the net assets and the capital is that the capital is what is invested in the business by the shareholders or proprietors. The concrete expression of that investment, in terms of assets and liabilities, is shown in more detail in the balance sheet.

Fixed assets
These are long-term assets of the business, consisting of tangible and intangible assets.

Tangible assets
These assets have a physical existence, as the name

suggests. They include things like land and buildings, plant and machinery, vehicles, etc.

Intangible assets
These are assets without a physical existence – such as goodwill, patents and so on.

Depreciation
All fixed assets are subject to depreciation. Depreciation is written off the value of fixed assets, spreading the cost of the assets over their useful lives.

Current assets
These are short-term assets, which by their nature change from day to day – even from hour to hour – in the course of business. They include things like the bank balance, debts, stock and expenses paid in advance.

Current liabilities
These are short-term liabilities of the business, changing from day to day, a counterpart to the current assets. They include bank overdrafts, current instalments on hire purchase contracts or loans, monies owing to creditors and accrued expenses. Current liabilities are generally recognised as those falling due within one year.

Working capital
The difference between current assets and current liabilities (net current assets) is known as working capital, considered in more detail in Chapter 5. If the current liabilities exceed the current assets, it is known as a working capital deficit. This would generally be indicative of an illiquid situation. A working capital deficit could

mean that the business is insolvent, although this is not necessarily always true.

Insolvency means that the business is unable to meet its current liabilities as they become due.

Long-term liabilities
These are liabilities due for payment after more than one year. They include things like long-term loans and later instalments on loans and hire purchase contracts.

Net assets
This is simply the net sum of all the assets less the liabilities of the business. If the total liabilities exceed the total assets, then the business has net liabilities. It is also, of course, a sign of financial weakness, at the very least, and could indicate the financial collapse of the business.

COMPARISONS

The figures do not exist independently of anything else. They are at their most useful when shown in comparison with something.

The most common comparisons are with corresponding previous periods and with budgeted figures.

The comparison with previous periods will show what progress or otherwise has been made, and trends. Trends may be indicative of growth or decline, or they may follow cyclical patterns. These patterns may mirror the economy of the country generally, or they may be peculiar to the specific trade or industry.

The comparison with budgets will show how far plans and targets have been achieved. We consider budgets in more detail in Chapter 4.

Internal comparisons show the relationships of various figures to each other.

STATISTICAL ANALYSIS AND KEY RATIOS

Certain key ratios and relationships can be measured by comparing different figures within the set of accounts. These provide useful pointers to improving business performance and profitability. Detailed examination of key ratios and relationships often leads to more searching questions about various areas of business performance.

The key ratios shown here will be illustrated by reference to the specimen financial statements shown in Figure 2.2, which is an expanded form of the same information given in Figure 2.1. The extra column shows the budget figures for the current year. The reference letters on each line to the right of the current year figures are used for identification in the explanations below.

Profit ratios

Gross profit percentage
One of the most important ratios for any business, of whatever type, is the ratio of the gross profit to the sales (or turnover). It can be adapted to manufacturing, wholesale, retail, and even service businesses.

Profit and loss account

	Current year £000	Current year £000		Previous year £000	Previous year £000	Budget £000	Budget £000
Sales		500	a		450		550
Cost of sales							
Materials	150		b	120		150	
Direct labour	100		c	80		110	
Factory costs	50		d	50		50	
		300	e		250		310
Gross profit		200	f		200		240
Other income		5			2		3
		205			202		243
Overheads							
Property	20		g	15		20	
Salaries	30		h	28		32	
Maintenance	10		i	12		12	
Administration	5		j	6		5	
Transport	10		k	11		9	
Marketing	10		l	9		10	
Depreciation	10		m	9		10	
Interest	15		n	14		15	
Total overheads		110	o		104		113
Net profit		95	p		98		130
Taxation	30		q	30		40	
Dividends	40		r	35		45	
		70			65		85
Retained profit		25	s		33		45
Balance sheet							
Fixed assets		400	t		350		390
Current assets							
Stock	40		u	35		45	
Work in progress	10		v	9		10	
Debtors	60		w	55		55	
Cash and bank	20		x	15		20	
	130		y	114		130	
Current liabilities							
Trade creditors	40		z	37		40	
Taxes	10		aa	8		12	
HP instalments	5		ab	6		4	
Overdraft	10		ac	8		5	
	65		ad	59		61	
Working capital		65	ae		55		69
Total assets less current liabilities		465			405		459
Long-term liabilities							
Loans		80	af		85		70
Net assets		385	ag		320		389
Capital							
Share capital							
Preference shares	50		ah	50		50	
Ordinary shares	100		ai	70		82	
	150		aj	120		132	
Share premium	10		ak			20	
		160	al		120		152
Profit and loss account		225	am		200		237
Shareholders' funds		385	an		320		389

Figure 2.2 Specimen company accounts for the year ended
31 December 20xx

The gross profit (f) is arrived at by deducting the cost of sales (e) from the sales turnover (a). The gross profit percentage is the gross profit (f) expressed as a percentage of the sales turnover (a). The formula is therefore:

$$\frac{f \times 100}{a}$$

In the example, the gross profit percentage is 40%, compared with 44.4% in the previous period and 43.6% in the budget.

The gross profit percentage can be further analysed to find out the reasons for any variations from the expected figure. There are several reasons for variations in gross profit percentage, including:

♦ *Sales mix.* The mix of products included in the total sales may have shown a variation which could affect the overall gross profit percentage because some items carry a higher profit mark-up than others. For example, a typical corner shop might sell tobacco products, confectionery, newspapers and greetings cards. The mark-up on tobacco would usually be much less than that on other items. Thus a change in the relative volumes of sales would affect the overall percentage.

♦ *Increased competition.* Competition may force price cuts with no corresponding cut in the cost of sales, adversely affecting the gross profit percentage.

♦ *Increased materials cost.* The cost of raw materials may have risen, with little or no chance of passing these increases on to customers by increasing sales prices.

Cost of sales analysis

Since the gross profit is arrived at by deducting the cost of sales from the sales turnover, it follows that the cost of sales expressed as a percentage of the sales turnover is complementary to the gross profit percentage. Thus, in our example, the current year's gross profit percentage is 40%, so the cost of sales percentage is 60%. The calculation is the cost of sales (e) as a percentage of the sales turnover (a). The formula is:

$$\frac{e \times 100}{a}$$

Where the cost of sales is made up of several items, the various components of the cost of sales can be compared separately. Thus, in our example, the total cost of sales is £300,000 or 60% of turnover. Further analysis can be carried out to show the relative percentages of materials, direct labour, and factory costs, yielding the following results:

	Percentage of sales		
	Current year	*Previous year*	*Budget*
	%	%	%
Materials (b × 100/a)	30	26.7	27.3
Direct labour (c × 100/a)	20	17.8	20
Factory costs (d × 100/a)	10	11.1	9.1

Each of these variations, particularly against the budgeted figures, can then be investigated. Most of the direct costs are variable – that is they vary in direct proportion to the sales. Therefore it would be expected that the percentage relationship of these items to the sales would remain constant. Thus where there is a significant variance – as in the above example, for materials cost – the cause should be investigated. The increase could be due to a volume variance or a cost variance compared with both the previous year and the budgeted figure.

A volume variance means that the amount of materials used, or paid for and not used, has varied. This could be due to some malfunction in the manufacturing process or other reasons such as wastage, loss or pilferage of materials.

A cost variance means that the same volume has cost more than either the previous year or the budgeted amount, and this should lead to steps being taken to control costs.

However, some of the direct costs also have an element of fixed cost, and this is particularly so in the case of direct labour and factory costs. The volume of sales may therefore affect these percentages. The control issues here are therefore different from the control of items which are fully variable.

This process of cost analysis provides an example of the principle already seen:

If you can't measure it, you can't control it.

Detailed gross profit analysis

The analysis of cost of sales and of gross profit margins may also be extended to cover more complex situations where there are different products, departments or sales lines.

Example 2.1

High Street Motor sales consist of the following elements:

- fuel and oil sales;
- new car sales;
- second-hand car sales;
- servicing and spares sales.

The various items of the sales and cost of sales are broken down into those categories to provide an analysis of the gross profit on each department. The analysis is illustrated in Figure 2.3. This analysis can be used to highlight areas in which the performance of the departments can be compared with one another for the current year, with the previous year's figures and with the budgeted figures.

Here are some suggestions of the issues raised by this analysis:

- Why was the overall gross profit lower in percentage terms and in absolute terms than both the previous year and the budget?

- Why was the gross profit on fuel sales so much lower than budgeted? Is there a possibility of a leak in the pumps or tanks?

- Why were new car sales not up to the budgeted figure, and why is the gross profit percentage less than both the budgeted figure and the previous year's figures? Does the dealership agreement with the car company need revision?

◆ Why did the second-hand car sales underperform in sales volume and profit rate? Does this underperformance reflect the abilities of the salespeople?

◆ Why did the servicing and spares department underperform in sales volume and profit rate compared with the budget? Could there be any inaccuracies in recording things like transfer of materials between departments?

◆ Is it worth continuing the fuel sales, given that they produce so little gross profit? Could the space taken up be better used for something else?

Net profit percentage

This calculation measures the net profit before tax and dividends or other distributions (line p in Figure 2.2) as a percentage of the sales. The formula is:

$$\frac{p \times 100}{a}$$

In this case, the figure is 19% compared with the previous year's percentage of 21.8% and the budgeted figure of 23.6%. The net profit percentage has many more variables than the gross profit percentage, so there will normally be a much greater variation in this figure.

The net profit percentage shows how much of each pound's worth of sales remains as profit after all expenses. However, tax has to be taken out of this figure and dividends can only be paid out of net profit.

Overheads percentage analysis

Measuring each overhead expense as a percentage of sales

Total figures	Current year £000	£000	Previous year £000	£000	Budget £000	£000
Sales		600		610		660
Cost of sales						
Materials	370		360		398	
Direct labour	78		75		75	
Direct costs	21		22		22	
		469		457		495
Gross profit		131		153		165
Gross profit percentage		21.8		25.1		25.0

Fuel sales	£000	£000	£000	£000	£000	£000
Sales		200		180		210
Cost of sales						
Materials	185		165		185	
Direct labour	3		3		3	
Direct costs	2		2		3	
		190		170		191
Gross profit		10		10		19
Gross profit percentage		5.0		5.6		9.0

New car sales	£000	£000	£000	£000	£000	£000
Sales		200		200		220
Cost of sales						
Materials	100		95		110	
Direct labour	6		6		5	
Direct costs	5		5		5	
		111		106		120
Gross profit		89		94		100
Gross profit percentage		44.5		47.0		45.5

Second-hand car sales	£000	£000	£000	£000	£000	£000
Sales		80		120		100
Cost of sales						
Materials	60		80		75	
Direct labour	4		6		5	
Direct costs	4		5		4	
		68		91		84
Gross profit		12		29		16
Gross profit percentage		15.0		24.2		16.0

Servicing and spares sales	£000	£000	£000	£000	£000	£000
Sales		120		110		130
Cost of sales						
Materials	25		20		28	
Direct labour	65		60		62	
Direct costs	10		10		10	
		100		90		100
Gross profit		20		20		30
Gross profit percentage		16.7		18.2		23.1

Figure 2.3. High Street Motors analysis of figures

can also be used to indicate possible areas of control. Thus, in Figure 2.2, the comparative overheads percentage analysis would look like this:

Overheads	Current year % of sales	Previous year % of sales	Budget % of sales
Property	4	3.3	3.6
Salaries	6	6.2	5.8
Maintenance	2	2.7	2.2
Administration	1	1.3	0.9
Transport	2	2.4	1.6
Marketing	2	2	1.8
Depreciation	2	2	1.8
Interest	3	3.1	2.7
Total overheads	22	23.1	20.5

The reasons for all variations should be explained. The explanations can lead to further examination of individual items making up each category of overheads.

It is not just the unfavourable variations that require explanation.

Example 2.2
Within the category of administration costs, the amount spent on insurance shows a favourable comparison with the budgeted figure. This should be examined to consider whether all aspects of the business are adequately insured. The insurance cost could be too low because the business does not have adequate cover. The amount of cover for each risk should be reviewed regularly, and the comparative costs of covering the risk should be reviewed at intervals to ensure value for money.

The nature of overheads
The nature of each type of overhead expense should also be borne in mind when examining variances. Some expenses, such as advertising or marketing, may have a budgeted cap and the department responsible must work within their budget. Any overspend on budgeted items such as this must be carefully investigated to see if any breach has occurred in internal controls.

Most overheads are fixed by their nature – that is, they are not directly variable in relation to sales. However, some overheads do have a variable element as well as a fixed element. For example, administrative salaries may well be fixed up to a certain point, but if there is a large expansion in operations, more administrative staff may be necessary. The same may be true of distribution and transport costs. The salaries of sales staff often include a fixed element of salary and an element of commission based on sales.

Return on capital employed
Return on capital employed (ROCE) is the net profit (before interest, tax and dividends) expressed as a percentage of the total capital employed in the business (i.e. including equity capital and loan capital). This ratio therefore measures the total returns to all suppliers of long-term finance, whether by loans or by equity capital.

In Figure 2.2, the formula is:

$$\frac{\text{Net profit plus interest} \times 100}{\text{Shareholders' capital plus long-term loans}}$$

or:

$$\frac{(p + n) \times 100}{(an + af)}$$

This calculation produces a figure of 23.7% for the current year, compared with 27.7% the previous year and 31.6% budgeted.

Return on investment

This is sometimes known as 'return on shareholders' funds' and is thus distinct from the ROCE. This is expressed as the percentage of net profit to shareholders' funds.

♦ The definition of net profit is the profit before tax and dividends.

♦ The definition of shareholders' funds is the equity capital plus reserves. Thus it excludes loan capital and therefore the result of this calculation is greatly affected by the gearing (see below).

In Figure 2.2, the formula is:

$$\frac{\text{Net profit} \times 100}{\text{Shareholders' capital}}$$

or:

$$\frac{p \times 100}{an}$$

This calculation produces a figure of 24.7% as the return on shareholders' funds for the current year. However, this has declined from 30.6% the previous year and the budgeted figure was 33.4%. Clearly some explanation is needed.

Liquidity ratios

Current ratio
This key ratio measures liquidity, which is closely akin to working capital, the management of which is dealt with in Chapter 5. The current ratio is simply the relationship between current assets and current liabilities. It is normally expressed as the fraction which current assets bears to current liabilities.

This calculation will arrive at a figure greater or less than one. If the current assets are greater than the current liabilities, the result will exceed one. If the current liabilities exceed the current assets, the result will be less than one.

In Figure 2.2, the calculation is:

$$\frac{\text{Current assets}}{\text{Current liabilities}}$$

or:

$$\frac{y}{ad}$$

The result of this is 2, meaning that the current assets are double the current liabilities. The previous year's ratio was 1.93. However, it was budgeted to have increased to 2.13.

If this ratio yields a figure of less than one, it might indicate some degree of illiquidity. However, some businesses such as supermarkets do manage to operate on a low ratio. This ratio is of the utmost importance, and trends must be monitored regularly.

Quick ratio
This is sometimes known as the 'acid test' ratio. Stock is excluded from the current assets and the quick ratio is therefore a measure of the immediately available monies, as a comparison with current liabilities.

This calculation will always result in a lower figure than the current ratio. However, the important aspect of this ratio is the trend. This ratio also gives a more sharply defined test of liquidity and solvency.

In Figure 2.2, this formula is:

$$\frac{\text{Current assets less stock and work in progress}}{\text{Current liabilities}}$$

or:

$$\frac{y-(u+v)}{ad}$$

The result of this is 1.23, compared with 1.18 the previous year and a budgeted ratio of 1.23.

Activity ratios
These ratios show the efficiency of the controls in relation to business activities, such as stock turnover and credit control.

Debtor days
This measures the debts outstanding on the sales ledger against the annual sales to arrive at a figure showing the

number of days' sales outstanding at any one point. In Figure 2.2, the calculation (assuming that all of the debtors are sales ledger debtors) is:

$$\frac{\text{Sales ledger debtors} \times 365}{\text{Annual sales}}$$

or:

$$\frac{w \times 365}{a}$$

The result is 43.8. Thus there are, at the balance sheet date, 44 days' sales outstanding (to the nearest day). The previous year's figure was 45 days, and the budgeted figure was 36 days. However, this measure only shows the picture at one specific date. To get a better picture, the same calculation could be carried out at different dates and regularly throughout the year. This shows trends and whether the situation is improving or declining.

Creditor days

This measures how much credit is being taken from suppliers. It is calculated from the trade creditors figure (z in Figure 2.2) compared with the total purchase ledger items in the year (which is not shown in Figure 2.2) and multiplied by 365. Although not shown in these accounts, the total purchase ledger items can be arrived at by addition of the monthly totals in the purchase daybook. Once again, this only shows the position at a specific date. The same calculation could also be carried out at different dates and regularly throughout the year.

Trends are important, and a lengthening trend could indicate infringement of normal authorised trade terms with suppliers. If this were allowed to continue, it could endanger working relationships with suppliers and lead to shortages of vital supplies. The whole production cycle could be disrupted, with a serious effect on the viability of the business.

Stock turnover
This measures the number of times that stock is turned over during the year. It is measured by dividing the cost of materials used by the closing stock and work in progress figure. In Figure 2.2, this calculation is:

$$\frac{\text{Cost of materials}}{\text{Stock and work in progress}}$$

or:

$$\frac{b}{u+v}$$

The result of this calculation is 3 times in the current year, 2.7 times in the previous year and budgeted 2.7 times. In general, higher stock turnover indicates better stock control procedures.

This method can be refined, by using the average level of stock carried throughout the year as the basis of comparison. This can be arrived at by averaging out the opening stock and work in progress and the closing stock and work in progress. Thus, in Figure 2.2, the figure to use would be the average of the previous year's figures and the current year's figures, which gives £47,000 instead of £50,000. This yields a stock turnover figure of 3.2 times.

If the stock records provide monthly stock and work in progress figures, it is also possible to use the average of the twelve months' figures to give an even more accurate stock turnover. This exercise can then be carried out on a 'rolling year' basis. This means that every month, the figure used is the average of the preceding twelve months and the stock turnover is worked out on the cost of materials over the previous twelve months.

A decreasing stock turnover trend could point to dangers of stock deterioration, wastage, pilferage or obsolescence.

There can be no absolute guide to ideal stock turnover figures. The figures vary greatly from one business to another. Manufacturing businesses, for example, generally turn stock over more slowly than retail businesses. Even different types of retail businesses turn stock over at different rates. Fashion retailers, for instance, would carry larger volumes of stock than fast-food outlets or fresh food retailers.

Asset turnover
This is a calculation, or rather a series of calculations, to show the sales generated by the assets used, either the fixed assets, the total gross assets or the net assets. Once again, these figures are best seen as comparisons with previous periods to recognise trends. They point to the efficiency of asset management and use.

Fixed asset turnover
In Figure 2.2, the fixed asset turnover can be calculated by the formula:

$$\frac{\text{Turnover}}{\text{Total fixed assets}}$$

or:

$$\frac{a}{t}$$

This shows £500,000 of turnover generated by £400,000 of fixed assets – a ratio of 1.25, compared with 1.28 the previous year and the budgeted figure of 1.41. This means that every £1 of fixed assets generates £1.25 of sales for the current year, £1.28 of sales the previous year and £1.41 of budgeted sales. This can be broken down further and the turnover applied to different types of fixed assets.

The comparisons for fixed asset turnover can be distorted when there is significant investment in new assets.

Gross asset turnover
In Figure 2.2, the gross asset turnover can be calculated by the formula:

$$\frac{\text{Turnover}}{\text{Total fixed assets plus total current assets}}$$

or:

$$\frac{a}{t+y}$$

This gives a ratio of 0.95 compared with 0.97 the previous year and a budget of 1.06.

Net asset turnover

In Figure 2.2, the net asset turnover can be calculated by the formula:

$$\frac{\text{Turnover}}{\text{Net assets}}$$

or:

$$\frac{a}{ag}$$

This shows a ratio of 1.30 the current year, 1.40 the previous year and a budget of 1.41.

Capital ratios

Total liabilities to total assets

An important figure in the balance sheet is the net assets (ag in Figure 2.2), showing the actual figure represented by the shareholders' funds. The details show how it is made up between assets and liabilities, and the breakdown between long-term and short-term assets and liabilities.

Another useful ratio figure is the ratio between total liabilities and total assets. In Figure 2.2, this is calculated by the formula:

$$\frac{\text{Current liabilities plus long-term liabilities}}{\text{Fixed assets plus current assets}}$$

or:

$$\frac{ad + af}{t + y}$$

In the example, the ratio arrived at is 0.27 compared with 0.31 the previous year and a budget of 0.25.

This can also be broken down to the short-term liabilities against short-term assets, and long-term liabilities against long-term assets. This is calculated by, for short-term figures:

$$\frac{\text{Current liabilities}}{\text{Current assets}}$$

or:

$$\frac{ad}{y}$$

and for long-term figures:

$$\frac{\text{Long-term liabilities}}{\text{Fixed assets}}$$

or:

$$\frac{af}{t}$$

The short-term ratio figure is therefore 0.5 for the current year and 0.5 for the previous year with a budget figure of 0.47. (This is the reverse of the current ratio above.) The long-term figure is 0.2 for the current year, 0.24 for the previous year, and 0.18 budgeted.

Gearing

Gearing represents the relationship of loan capital to total capital. If a company has long-term loans of £800,000 and equity capital of £200,000, the total capital is £1,000,000. The percentage of loans to total capital is

80%. In general terms, anything above 50% is considered a high gearing, although each case must be considered on its own merit.

In Figure 2.2, the calculation is:

$$\frac{\text{Long-term liabilities} \times 100}{\text{Long-term liabilities plus shareholders' funds}}$$

or:

$$\frac{\text{af} \times 100}{\text{af} + \text{an}}$$

This calculation reveals a gearing of 18%.

Gearing is considered in further detail in Chapter 10, where it will be seen that high gearing is more risky for equity investors. A crucial factor in a high-geared company is interest cover.

Interest cover
This is a particular measure of one specific item of overhead – interest paid on loans. It shows how the interest paid relates to the profit. In Figure 2.2, the calculation is:

$$\frac{\text{Net profit}}{\text{Interest}}$$

or:

$$\frac{\text{p}}{\text{n}}$$

This calculation shows interest cover of 6 times compared with 6.8 times the previous year and a budgeted figure of 8.5 times.

The significance of this figure is shown if profits should drop. If a business has a low interest cover, any drop in profits means that, after interest is paid, the amount available for distribution as dividends is much lower. This is more pronounced in businesses which are highly geared.

SUMMARY

Financial accounts, cost accounts and management accounts are the raw material of financial control and management.

Understanding them is a key to the effective management of the finances of any business.

Understanding financial statements is an indispensable tool in financial management. However, it is not enough simply to look at the accounts and understand what they mean. Understanding must be followed by action, and that action is the essence of financial management.

Experience is also important in exercising control. When financial directors or managers have been working in the same business for some time, experience of the business will enable them to spot trends or anomalies in the figures – it becomes a kind of instinct.

Example 2.3

♦ An analysis of the activity ratios may show that the quick ratio has been steady for the last six months. In itself, this may appear satisfactory.

- However, over the same period, the debor days have increased, from 36 days six months ago to 39 days at present.

- This could indicate that something is slipping in the sales ledger department – perhaps the control procedures are becoming more lax.

- Procedures should be looked at. Are they being applied consistently? Have there been staff changes in the sales ledger department affecting the credit control procedures? Are new customers being accepted without the proper controls?

- An examination of the aged debtor lists for each month may show specific problems. Do the figures show a gradual increase month by month, or is there a sudden increase in one month which should be examined more carefully?

- Is any particular debtor or group of debtors showing delinquent behaviour, such as unauthorised extensions of their credit period? If so, has anyone contacted them? Are current orders on hold while the problem is sorted out?

However, even the most experienced financial managers can often overlook problems or solutions that another, less experienced, person may suggest. Therefore it is vital to remain open to any and all suggestions. Very often, something pointed out by a person from a different department can also enlighten a problem and lead to a successful course of action. Financial managers must be prepared to listen to non-financial managers and other employees lower down the line.

③

Financial Reporting

In this chapter we study the basics of reporting on the financial information, introducing you to:

- the external and internal reports which are commonly prepared for any business; and
- the effective presentation of reports and figures, including the use of graphical displays.

REPORTING – EXTERNAL AND INTERNAL

External reporting requirements

The periodic published accounts (which for limited companies have to be filed at Companies House) represent the external reporting requirements of a business. Any member of the public can inspect and obtain copies of accounts filed at Companies House.

Limited companies, partnerships and sole traders must prepare accounts from which to compile their self-assessment tax returns which are sent to the Inland Revenue. Not all accounts are examined, but the Inland Revenue examines a proportion of business accounts every year.

The Inland Revenue can also examine any aspect of the accounts in connection with PAYE audits. Although PAYE investigations are initially concerned with deductions made from employees and the payment of that money to the Inland Revenue, they can involve many areas of the business.

Customs and Excise, which administers VAT, also has the right to examine business accounts, and they arrange regular inspection visits.

Either the Inland Revenue or Customs and Excise can extend their enquiries into the accounting records of the business as well as the final accounts.

Basic accounting conventions

All external accounts of a business are expected to comply with certain basic accounting principles. These are as follows.

Accruals basis

This means that all income and expenditure should be matched to the period covered by the accounts, irrespective of when the actual payment or receipt occurred.

Historic cost

Business assets are normally shown at their original cost, less depreciation where applicable. In times of significant inflation, these original costs (known as historic costs) bear no relation to current costs or values. However, historic costs are probably the most objective ones to use in accounts.

Revaluation

If it is desired to adjust the historic costs to current costs to try to bring into account the effects of inflation, adjustments can be made by revaluing certain assets – generally the fixed assets. An adjustment must be made to the equity of the business by creating a revaluation reserve.

Materiality

This means disregarding items which are insignificant in relation to the accounts as a whole. This is clearly dependent on the size of the business. What is immaterial to British Telecom may not be immaterial to a small corner shop. The degree of materiality is shown by rounding figures to the nearest pound, or to the nearest million pounds.

Prudence

This concept can be summarised as 'erring on the safe side'. Thus, losses are recognised in the accounts as soon as they are reasonably foreseeable, while profits are only recognised in the accounts when they are actually realised.

Prudence also requires provisions to be made in the accounts for foreseeable but uncertain losses or expenses. If, for example, there is a court case pending at the date of the balance sheet of uncertain outcome, it is prudent to make a provision for the costs of the case if the decision should be unfavourable.

Provisions are commonly made for bad debts and discounts on sales ledger debts. It is usually not known exactly which customers will default on payment of their debts, but experience suggests that a certain percentage will prove to be bad. Therefore it is valid to make a general provision for bad and doubtful debts as a percentage of outstanding debts.

Similarly, it is not known how many and which customers will take advantage of any prompt payment discounts. Experience again suggests that a certain percentage will do so, and it is valid to make a general provision for this by reducing the debtors figure in the balance sheet.

Consistency

Business accounts must be consistent in their treatment of transactions – both within the accounting period and between one accounting period and another. This enables readers of the accounts to make proper and reasonable comparisons on which judgments may be based.

If a change in the treatment of transactions in the accounts is necessary, the reason must be explained. A note should explain the effect of this change and how the accounts of the previous year or period might have been affected if the change were implemented then. This enables a proper comparison to be made.

Going concern

This means that the accounts are prepared on the basis that the business will continue to carry on its business for the foreseeable future.

If a business is not a going concern, the assets must be included at their knockdown value – that is, what they could be reasonably expected to produce at auction. The inevitable losses produced by this must be shown in full.

Substance over form

This concept means that if the 'form' of a transaction suggests one thing but the substance of the transaction is different, the substance must be reflected in the accounts. This is an 'anti-avoidance' principle. A typical example is of assets that are leased rather than owned. If the lease is really a means of financing the purchase of the asset, it must be shown as an asset, and the liability created by the lease finance shown as a balance sheet liability. This is dealt with further in Chapter 10.

Official requirements

In addition to the above conventions, the accounts of limited companies must comply with the reporting requirements of the Companies Act and officially published Accounting Standards.

Internal reporting

External reports are published usually annually or half-yearly, and they can sometimes take several weeks to prepare. They are often then subject to audit and therefore they may not appear until some while after the end of the accounting period.

Internal reports are needed for various purposes within the business and are not published. They are used mainly for management purposes, and are therefore generally referred to as management accounts. Because these accounts are needed for making management decisions, they are prepared much more frequently – generally monthly, but sometimes even more frequently than that. They are also needed promptly.

While management figures should obviously be as accurate as possible, the degree of promptness is often an overriding factor. A common saying is:

> It is better to have management figures that are on time but only 95% accurate than to have them 100% accurate but a fortnight late.

These reports are tailored to specific needs and they can be produced in many formats. They are produced for different levels of management and for different departments or functions. They can be regular reports or specific one-off reports, such as an analysis of a particular project. They are concerned not with reporting the past but for present control and future forecasts.

BREAKEVEN ANALYSIS

Breakeven analysis is one example of internal reporting. It is a technique for discovering what volume of sales must be achieved for the business to meet all its costs before making a profit. This can be applied to the business as a whole or to divisions or departments.

This analysis requires a classification of costs into fixed and variable. Fixed costs are what the business will incur regardless of the volume of sales. Variable costs are those directly related to the sales.

If costs might include an element of fixed cost and an element of variable cost, they need further analysis to break them down into the variable element and the fixed element.

A typical breakeven analysis can be shown as a graph.

Example 3.1

Suppose that a business sells one item only and that the selling price of each item is £10 and the variable costs are £7, giving a direct (gross) profit of £3 on each article sold. If the fixed costs are £30,000, how many items must be sold to break even?

Figure 3.1. shows how this is represented in a graph. The break-even point is shown where the sales line intersects the total costs line. This occurs at a sales volume of 10,000. For any volume of sales the profit or loss is the difference between the sales line and the total costs line.

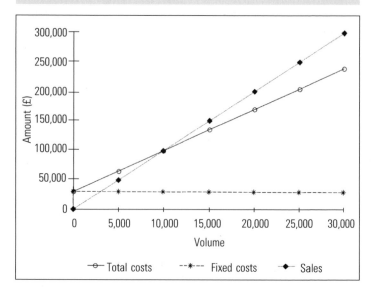

Figure 3.1. Breakeven chart

Example 3.2

In order to achieve a volume of 10,000 sales, the fixed costs would have to increase to £50,000, and to achieve a volume of 20,000 sales, the fixed costs would have to increase to £70,000. Suppose further that, as a result of these extra fixed costs, the variable costs of each article would reduce to £6 if sales exceed 10,000 volume, and to £5 if sales exceed 20,000 volume. Also, in order to achieve more than 10,000 volume sales, the price would need to be reduced to £9 per item, and to achieve more than 20,000 volume sales, the price would have to be reduced to £7.50. Here the answer is not so obvious at first sight, and further use of the graph is needed as shown in Figure 3.2.

The result here shows that the profile is quite different. There are three points of intersection of the sales and total costs, at volumes of about 17,000, 23,000 and 28,000. These are points at which breakeven occurs. There are intermediate points where the net result is a profit or a loss, i.e. where the sales line is above or below the total costs line.

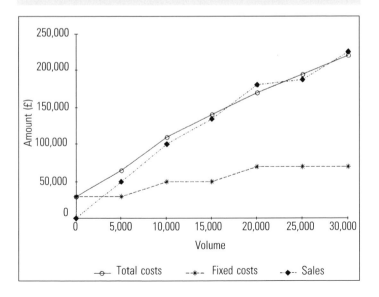

Figure 3.2 Breakeven chart.

Where several different products are involved, separate breakeven charts can be prepared for each product, with fixed expenses being allocated among the different products. This type of chart can show which products are profitable, and which are not. However, the exercise would have to be recalculated if any particular product were discontinued and taken out of the analysis, because there would have to be a new allocation of fixed expenses so that they are all absorbed into this process.

Marginal cost analysis

The concept of marginal cost relates to the additional cost incurred to increase sales or production by a given amount. This analysis can easily be carried out by the application of the breakeven analysis and graph. The example in Figure 3.2 above illustrates this principle. For production up to 10,000 items, the marginal cost of each additional unit is equal to the variable cost, i.e. the materials and the direct labour. However, above 10,000 items, the marginal cost increases by the £20,000 additional fixed costs, offset by the reduction in variable costs due to economies of scale. Similar principles apply when the volume reaches 20,000 units.

The construction of the graph illustrates this process and enables the marginal costs to be plotted.

EFFECTIVE PRESENTATION OF FIGURES

Words and figures

Unless you can get across ideas or reasons for recommendations, much of your work will be fruitless. The use of words, oral or written, is at least as important as the ability to produce figures.

In some reports, figures may be relegated to an appendix. The inclusion of a table or column of figures can interrupt the flow of an argument or presentation of facts. Putting all the figures in appendices can make a report clearer, as long as there is adequate reference to them in the body of the text.

There can be no one solution to fit every report. Each report must be judged on its own merits and designed appropriately, bearing in mind the background of the readers.

Using significant figures

Large company accounts round figures to the nearest million. This avoids long strings of numbers, and makes the figures easier to understand. When reporting verbally, it can be more effective to tell someone that they made 'almost £370,000 profit' rather than saying that they made '£369,469 profit'. The rounding off level depends of course on the size of the enterprise.

Highlighting

Reports are sometimes presented as a dense block of rows and columns of figures. Even when the description of the figures is clearly shown, their significance may not be obvious at first sight. Even without any words, however, figures could be presented to highlight the important features.

Example 3.3

Figure 3.3 shows the analysis of overhead expenses of three branches of a firm. It is perfectly valid, but it is a solid block of figures. To get any more meaningful information from it, the figures would have to be examined and more work done on them. Figure 3.4 shows the same figures with the items more than 10% over budget highlighted. This immediately shows the items needing further examination. Highlighting could be done on any other basis – say, all items which were under budget could be highlighted.

	London branch		Leeds branch		Glasgow branch	
	Actual	Budget	Actual	Budget	Actual	Budget
Salaries	34,685	30,000	25,684	27,000	37,786	38,000
National Insurance	4,162	3,600	3,082	3,240	4,434	4,560
TOTAL	38,847	33,600	28,766	30,240	42,220	42,560
Rent and rates	17,893	14,000	12,364	12,300	18,256	18,500
Insurance	2,689	2,800	1,687	1,700	3,120	3,100
Light and heat	5,986	5,500	4,837	4,700	6,135	6,300
Repairs	686	1,500	5,900	1,000	523	1,500
TOTAL	27,254	23,800	24,788	19,700	28,034	29,400
Equipment maintenance	1,525	1,500	2,543	1,300	1,856	1,900
Equipment hire	1,200	1,200	1,000	100	1,200	1,200
TOTAL	2,725	2,700	3,543	1,400	3,056	3,100
Printing and stationery	1,586	1,400	1,234	1,110	1,867	1,950
Advertising	450	400	899	600	965	600
Telephone	1,432	1,450	1,323	1,200	1,963	1,750
Postage	986	800	565	650	866	890
Professional fees	2,534	2,200	1,852	1,900	2,132	2,400
Sundries	865	750	653	600	743	750
TOTAL	7,853	7,000	6,526	6,050	8,536	8,340
Bank charges	869	500	768	860	637	500
Bank interest	345	400	864	750	653	700
Loan interest	1,689	1,500	1,325	1,300	1,453	1,450
Credit card charges	1,897	1,300	1,659	1,400	1,863	1,600
TOTAL	4,800	3,700	4,616	4,310	4,606	4,250
GRAND TOTAL	81,479	70,800	68,239	61,700	86,452	87,650

Figure 3.3. Overheads comparison year ended 31 December 20xx

	London branch		Leeds branch		Glasgow branch	
	Actual	Budget	Actual	Budget	Actual	Budget
Salaries	34,685	30,000	25,684	27,000	37,786	38,000
National Insurance	4,162	3,600	3,082	3,240	4,434	4,560
TOTAL	38,847	33,600	28,766	30,240	42,220	42,560
Rent and rates	17,893	14,000	12,364	12,300	18,256	18,500
Insurance	2,689	2,800	1,687	1,700	3,120	3,100
Light and heat	5,986	5,500	4,837	4,700	6,135	6,300
Repairs	686	1,500	5,900	1,000	523	1,500
TOTAL	27,254	23,800	24,788	19,700	28,034	29,400
Equipment maintenance	1,525	1,500	2,543	1,300	1,856	1,900
Equipment hire	1,200	1,200	1,000	100	1,200	1,200
TOTAL	2,725	2,700	3,543	1,400	3,056	3,100
Printing and stationery	1,586	1,400	1,234	1,110	1,867	1,950
Advertising	450	400	899	600	965	600
Telephone	1,432	1,450	1,323	1,200	1,963	1,750
Postage	986	800	565	650	866	890
Professional fees	2,534	2,200	1,852	1,900	2,132	2,400
Sundries	865	750	653	600	743	750
TOTAL	7,853	7,000	6,526	6,050	8,536	8,340
Bank charges	869	500	768	860	637	500
Bank interest	345	400	864	750	653	700
Loan interest	1,689	1,500	1,325	1,300	1,453	1,450
Credit card charges	1,897	1,300	1,659	1,400	1,863	1,600
TOTAL	4,800	3,700	4,616	4,310	4,606	4,250
GRAND TOTAL	81,479	70,800	68,239	61,700	86,452	87,650

Figure 3.4. Overheads comparison year ended 31 December 20xx

Graphic reporting

It is said that a picture is worth a thousand words. Much financial information can be presented graphically, as well as, or instead of, in figures. Statutory reports must be presented in the right format and must comply with various regulations. However, other information can also be presented. Many large companies produce their annual report and accounts in glossy formats, replete with photographs of the company's business at work, with charts and graphs to emphasise the importance of certain key figures.

Graphic presentation can also be used for internal reports. We saw how a line chart (or graph) can be the best way of presenting a breakeven analysis.

Line charts (graphs)

These are perhaps the most recognisable and understood types of chart. We saw its use in breakeven analysis. That showed three lines on the chart and the important thing was the relationship between them. Single line charts can also be effective – displayed, say, on the wall of an office or workshop, they can be an incentive to achieve targets.

Bar charts

Figure 3.5 gives an illustration of a bar chart. This shows the comparisons of the actual overheads of each branch with the budget for each branch. This type of chart serves best for comparisons between different elements.

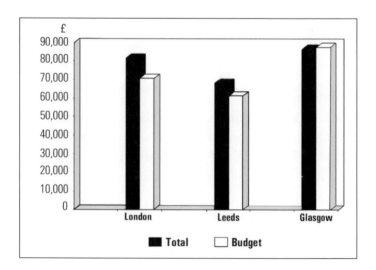

Figure 3.5. Overheads budget comparison

Pie charts

These are useful for showing the proportions of a total represented by each constituent part. Figure 3.6 gives an illustration of this showing the breakdown of the total overheads for London branch between the different categories of overheads.

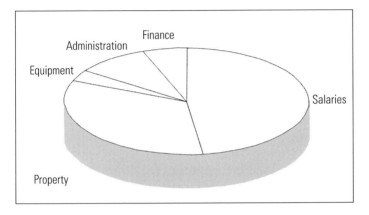

Figure 3.6 London branch overheads

Exercise 3.1

From the data in Figure 3.7, decide which form of graphic representation is best suited to show the following, then prepare the appropriate form of graph or chart for each one:

(a) the month by month debtors figures, showing the trend;

(b) the actual debtors figures each month compared with the forecast figures;

(c) the proportions of debtors analysed by age at July and December 20xx, for comparison.

What do these figures tell you about the debtors, and how do the graphs and charts emphasise the findings?

	Actual £	Forecast £
July	60,000	55,000
August	60,500	55,000
September	61,000	54,000
October	61,000	54,000
November	62,000	54,500
December	65,000	54,000

Age analysis of debtors:

	Up to 1 month £	1–2 months £	2–3 months £	over 3 months £
July	40,000	15,000	30,000	2,000
August	40,000	14,000	4,000	2,500
September	41,000	14,000	3,500	2,500
October	40,500	13,000	4,000	3,500
November	40,000	13,500	4,000	4,500
December	39,000	15,000	6,000	5,000

Figure 3.7. Sample data – debtors summary and analysis
for the six months ended 31 December 20xx

Suggested answer

The appropriate charts are:

(a) line chart (graph) – see Figure 3.8;

(b) bar chart – see Figure 3.9;

(c) pie charts – see Figures 3.10 and 3.11;

The figures represent a gradually worsening debtors position. The amounts owing are gradually increasing month by month and compared with the forecasts. The age analysis comparison shows that the age profile of the debts has deteriorated between July and December, and there is a much higher proportion of older debts outstanding at December.

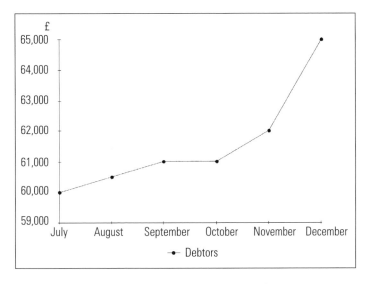

Figure 3.8. Debtors July to December

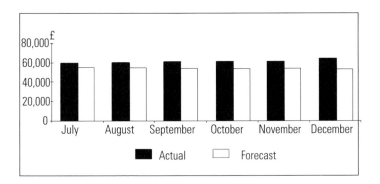

Figure 3.9 Comparison of actual/forecast debtors

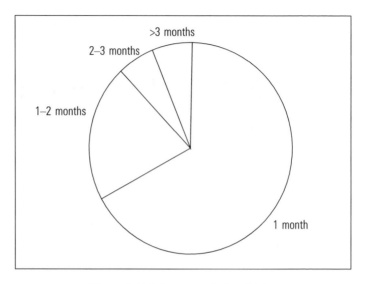

Figure 3.10 July age analysis of debts

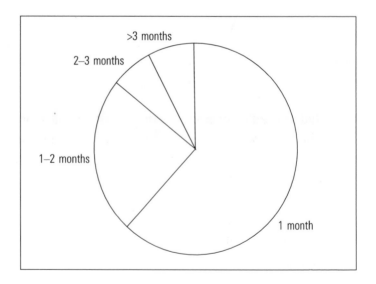

Figure 3.11 December age analysis of debts

The Budgeting Process

In this chapter, we look at the use of budgets to control the finances of a business. The importance of setting targets, and the human dimension of motivation is an integral part of the budgeting process. Results must be monitored against budgets, and we look at taking action based on the comparison of actual results to budgeted results. Another related tool is the SWOT analysis.

THE BUDGETING CYCLE

The point of budgeting is control. The budgeting process must result in effective control over the financial aspect of the business.

Budgets can incur a significant cost. If you have prepared a budget – perhaps for the bank when requesting finance – do not put it in a drawer and forget it. If it is forgotten as soon as it is formulated, it is worse than useless.

The budgeting process consists of several steps, and is a continuous circle. The process can be visualised as in Figure 4.1.

MAKING PLANS
Step one is to formulate plans providing a financial model

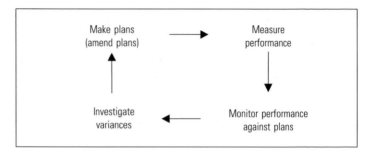

Figure 4.1. The budgeting process.

of the way the business will run. This involves obtaining reliable estimates from all departments of things such as sales, production, costs, overheads, capital expenditure and so on. Budgets are first prepared covering each department of the business individually, then amalgamated into an overall budget.

Budgets can also be prepared for new projects or ventures, as well as for existing core business. Budgets and plans for existing businesses start from the basis of the existing figures – what happened last year and how might that change? A budget for a new venture starts with no previous data – known as zero-based budgeting. The plans are not guided by past history but start from scratch.

The concept of zero-based budgeting can be extended to planning and budgeting for an existing business. It allows you to ask basic questions, such as 'Do we really need to produce the same product in the same way as at present, in the same premises?'

Usually, the key figure for the operating budget is the sales forecast, which the sales department traditionally makes optimistic. Attention must be given to judging its practicality and realism. The nature of the forecast sales must be taken into account. For example, if the sales department forecasts quite realistically a large volume of one-off or short-term sales, you cannot base a long-term expansion of productive capacity on that forecast.

The human dimension

Plans and budgets must be understood and agreed by the people whose job it is to meet those budgets. Thus budgeting is effective when the plans are prepared from the bottom-up rather than from the top-down. Failure here means that those who should be aiming to meet the budgets actually see them as the enemy rather than a tool for control. Therefore break down the budget into sections coming under the control of individual managers of departments.

Involve managers in the process of formulating the plans. To make the plans effective, managers should:

- ◆ agree their budget targets;
- ◆ believe that their targets are achievable;
- ◆ receive their budgets in a form relevant to their work; and
- ◆ receive training in understanding the budgets and their place in the wider overall purpose.

Motivation

Budgets can be an excellent tool for motivating people to

improve performance. If budgets are used as the basis for awarding bonuses, they must not be set so that they can be beaten and a bonus ensured. It is an unhealthy sign if budgets are always beaten. However, consistently setting budgets at a level too high to be met is a disincentive to better performance.

Managers of cost-centres or profit-centres will 'fight their own corner' to protect their patch and get what they see as their fair share of resources. Managers must be enabled to see the whole picture – how they contribute to the strategy of the business as a whole.

MEASURING PERFORMANCE

We have already seen this key concept:

accurate measurement of achievement is vital for the control process.

Information gleaned from the bookkeeping records usually provides the measurement needed for control. However, in some cases, other information is needed. For instance, production is measured in terms of the number of items produced rather than the money value attaching to those items. The production manager controls the production of goods, not the price at which they are sold. Therefore he needs to know the actual number of items produced, not the monetary value.

Similarly, the sales department is responsible for getting orders. Their measure is the orders received. If for any reason the production has not been able to satisfy those orders, that is not the sales department's responsibility.

Each department and profit centre should therefore have a system for recording actual achievement so that it can be compared to the budget.

The figures for these purposes should be produced regularly and promptly. For effective control, the figures should not be produced less than monthly, and in some cases weekly or fortnightly figures could be called for.

Control is effective when it is instigated immediately.

Service businesses

Service-based businesses have different financial measures for their output. Many businesses also sell a combination of goods and services.

Service businesses cannot store up their services as a manufacturing business can produce and stockpile its products. For example, if rooms in a hotel are empty for one night, that night's income is lost forever.

Thus different performance measures have to be devised. In the case of hotels, for example, the key measure is the occupancy rate. This means comparing the actual number of bed-nights' accommodation sold with the maximum possible if every bed were occupied every night, resulting in an occupancy percentage.

MONITORING PERFORMANCE AGAINST PLANS

Once figures are produced they can be compared with the budget. A simple budget comparison report should be produced for each cost centre, profit centre or department. For example, a typical part of a report for factory costs might look like Figure 4.2.

Budget report	Department	Date	Period	Prepared by
	....	....	....	....
Cost items	*Budget*	*Actual*	*Variance*	*Comments*
Machine operators' wages	£10,000	£12,000	+£2,000	Excessive overtime due to quality problems
Foremen's wages	£2,000	£2,400	+£400	Holiday cover overtime
Machinery repairs	£1,000	£500	−£500	New machinery resulted in lower repairs cost
Power supply	£2,000	£2,200	+£200	Additional operating time due to quality problems

Figure 4.2. Typical budget report for factory costs

The report should be the responsibility of the person most nearly responsible for meeting the budget figures. That person is the best qualified to make comments, particularly in explaining variances. The person responsible for meeting the budget should not feel that they are being hit over the head with the budget report, nor that it is just another piece of useless paperwork. It should be seen as a tool for improving performance, perhaps linked to a bonus or incentive.

INVESTIGATING VARIANCES

Variances from budgeted figures must be investigated,
so that action may be taken to control costs and income.

The budget report illustrated in Figure 4.2 gives the variances and the comments of the person preparing it. These comments may explain the variance or further investigation may be needed. Once the explanation is satisfactory, action can be determined.

Figures needing investigation must be prioritised. This could be done by highlighting all variances over a certain amount – for instance, anything more than 10% over budget gets investigated first.

It is not just the budget overruns which need investigating. Sometimes if a cost is below budget, the reason might bring to light some underlying cause affecting the rest of the business. For instance, the light, heat and power cost in a factory might be below budget because there has been a breakdown of machinery causing production to grind to a halt.

The reasons for variances may or may not lead to any action being taken. There may be alternative courses of action.

Example 4.1

The budget comparison report shows that the cost of the raw material for manufacture of an item shows a considerable increase as a percentage of the selling price. This raw material is bought from one supplier, who has raised his prices. Further investigation is needed. Why has the supplier raised his prices? If the prices have been raised ahead of his competition, consideration should be given to switching suppliers. However, the price increase may be general, due to a lack of world supply. In this case, switching to a new supplier is of no use, since all suppliers will be raising their prices. The decision must be taken whether the increase in costs can be absorbed or whether to pass it on to customers.

AMENDING PLANS

Action can only be taken when:

♦ the actual figures and achievements have been measured; and

♦ compared against budget; and

♦ the reason for any variances ascertained.

For instance, in Example 4.1 above, if the price increase is passed on to customers, the budgets need to be amended for the revised selling price, which will affect sales, and the revised buying price of the raw material, which will affect raw materials cost. The gross profit margin may or may not be the same as previously, and the original plan may have to be amended. If there is some basic flaw in the original plans and budget figures, it is obvious that they have to be amended.

Other things outside the control of the business change and these could affect the operation of the business.

For example, when the foot and mouth epidemic hit the UK in 2001, many businesses besides agriculture were seriously affected. Agriculture-related businesses and tourism-related businesses were affected and had to amend their plans and budgets.

The amended plans and budgets then replace the original ones, and the whole cycle starts again.

TIMESCALE

A year is a readily appreciable timescale, and one that fits in with accounting information. Yearly figures can be broken down into monthly or quarterly figures which can then be regularly monitored.

However, it is often necessary to look further ahead and make long-term plans – say for the next three, five or even ten years. These extended periods cannot be planned for and budgeted in such detail as a twelve-month period. These budgets adopt a more 'broad brush' approach.

Objectives and goals

In making long-term plans, the objectives and goals of the business must be examined, to see how they fit into long-term plans. The objectives of a business do not just have a financial aspect. They include many non-financial aspects, such as the type of market the business is aiming for.

The way in which objectives are met can be quite different. For example, production can be labour-intensive or highly mechanised.

All these circumstances translate differently into the financial plans and budgets. The long-term objectives, when laid out over an extended period of, say, five years, point to items such as the timing of major capital investment in premises or plant and machinery.

Product or service life cycle

The implications of the phases of a product or service life cycle are important. This applies to existing activities and any proposed new activities. The market for any product or service generally has four distinct phases, as shown in Figure 4.3.

1. *Introduction.*	This is generally associated with low sales, and high initial costs – therefore not very profitable.
2. *Growth.*	New suppliers of the product or service emerge into the market – greater competition is experienced.
3. *Maturity.*	The suppliers start to make better profits. Relatively few new suppliers are coming into the market.
4. *Decline.*	No new suppliers are coming into the market, but those already established in the market can continue to make profits until the demand has completely dried up.

Figure 4.3. Product life cycle

The greatest overall return comes when you get into the market as near as possible to the beginning of the life cycle. Any new venture may well incur high development costs. Therefore, aim to develop new products or services when there are existing income streams from other products or services.

You will be less vulnerable to fluctuating market demand if you have a range of products or services in different phases of the market life cycle.

SWOT ANALYSIS

When working out the details of how the objectives will be achieved over the long term, a SWOT analysis shows your Strengths, Weaknesses, Opportunities and Threats.

The strengths and weaknesses are internal to the business and are therefore much more controllable. The opportunities and threats are external to the business and are therefore less controllable. All of these elements – strengths, weaknesses, opportunities and threats – can be related to several areas of the business functions. Vital questions must be asked. A SWOT analysis must be searching and probing. Figure 4.5 shows some of the questions that could be asked. There are only four ways a business may increase its sales, derived from the matrix shown in Figure 4.4.

New products or services	New customers
Existing products or services	Existing customers

Figure 4.4. The four methods of increasing sales

Internal factors – strengths and weaknesses

Sales
◆ What patterns are emerging? Does the past record indicate any shift in demand for the products or services of the business? What is the profitability of different sales lines? Is any different mix of product and service indicated?
◆ Is there any customer feedback on the quality of products and services?
◆ What is the most convenient way of increasing sales? Figure 4.5 shows the four methods of increasing sales. The business must decide which of these is the most appropriate.

Customers
◆ Is the customer base changing?
◆ What are the real needs of the target group of customers?
◆ Can the business provide any other product or service to add value to the customers' business or private lives?

Competitors
◆ How does competitors' pricing structure compare?
◆ What special promotions do they carry out?
◆ Is their advertising enticing away any of the business's customers?
◆ What is their reputation in the marketplace?
◆ How easy or difficult is it for any new competitors to break into the market?

Supplies
◆ How secure are supplies of raw materials and other essentials?
◆ Are they dependent on world supply levels?
◆ Is there more than one supplier for each major item?

Management and administration
◆ Is there any shortage of staff or skills in any individual area?
◆ Are training facilities adequate?
◆ Are there any key employees without obvious successors?
◆ Would any planned changes create shortages of staff or skills?
◆ Would the organisational structure need changing?

Premises and equipment
◆ Will additional resources need to be made available?
◆ If so, when and where?
◆ Are the current premises suitable for any planned new activity?
◆ What finance will any new premises or equipment require?

Figure 4.5 Typical questions for a SWOT analysis

Financial resources

◆ Is the current activity adequately financed, or is there a shortage?

◆ What are the options for financing expansion?

◆ Can the management of working capital be improved in any area (see Chapter 5)?

External factors – opportunities and threats

Social factors

◆ There are always complex demographic, social and cultural forces at work in any society. How is the business affected by these influences? The effects could be felt in sales demand, in the availability of labour or in the general economic forces.

Technology

◆ What changes in technology are making the most impact on business in general currently?

◆ Which changes affect this business, and how?

◆ Technological changes are occurring with ever greater speed and make a fundamental impact on many areas of business. They can change demand, create demand for new products or services and affect the way business works – in production, in communications and in managing cash and capital.

The economy

◆ Many facets of the economy can affect the business – inflation, wage rates, legislation, tax rates, interest rates, foreign currency exchange rates.

Political factors

◆ Political stability can never be guaranteed – and this applies to some countries more than others.

◆ Could any political or legal changes affect the business?

Competition

◆ What is the size and influence of major competitors?

◆ What are their strengths and weaknesses, threats and opportunities?

◆ How easy is it for customers of the business to obtain substitutes for the business's products or services?

The market

◆ What is the size of the overall market in which the business sells its products or services?

◆ Is that market expanding or contracting?

◆ What is the size of the business's market share?

◆ Is that share expanding or contracting?

◆ Are any businesses in this market merging or forming alliances?

THE BOTTOM LINE

Budgets are only useful if they assist in controlling and planning the business. If they only tell you what happened last month, they are like the annual accounts serving that purpose for the last year.

Budgets must contribute to effective action.
Further, budgets can provide incentives to managers to perform.

However, they must be seen to encourage performance in absolute terms. It is not just performing to the budget that matters, but optimising profits and value.

TARGETS

Budgets are more about the future than about past performance.
Thus budgeting must be integrated with the other key management areas of the business.

Much current thinking is leading to setting of targets which are not expressed in monetary terms, but in measurable terms which are relevant and important to the business as a whole and to any particular area of management or department of the business.

This approach means that non-financial managers set many of the targets. Financial managers must be able to understand their language, and work in terms other than money figures. Managers must be able to identify the really important criteria and financial managers must cooperate with them in identifying and quantifying those measures.

Controlling Working Capital

One of the most important aspects of financial control is the control of working capital. We look individually at the nature of the various elements of working capital, working capital as a whole, and the ways to measure and control working capital.

WHAT IS WORKING CAPITAL?

Any business has assets and liabilities. The total capital of the business is represented by this formula:

Total assets minus total liabilities = Net assets = Total capital

as shown in Figure 5.1.

	£
Assets	500,000
Liabilities	200,000
Net assets	300,000
Capital	
Shares	100,000
Reserves	200,000
Total capital	300,000

Figure 5.1 ABC Ltd: Balance sheet

But total capital is not the same as working capital. To discover the working capital of a business, the assets and liabilities are broken down into long-term and short-term items. These are generally referred to by conventional names:

- long-term assets – fixed assets;
- short-term assets – current assets;
- long-term liabilities – long-term liabilities;
- short-term liabilities – current liabilities.

The division between short term and long term is one year. Thus money owed to the bank, repayable within one year, is a short-term (or current) liability.

To illustrate this, we can break down the figures from Figure 5.1 as in Figure 5.2.

	£	£
Fixed assets	300,000	
Current assets	200,000	
Total assets		500,000
Long-term liabilities	120,000	
Current liabilities	80,000	
Total liabilities		200,000
Net assets		300,000

Figure 5.2

This shows how the figures are divided between long-term and short-term items. A further step then shows what working capital is. This involves grouping together the short-term items (assets and liabilities) and showing them separately from the long-term items. This is conventionally shown as in Figure 5.3.

	£	£
Fixed assets		300,000
Current assets	200,000	
Current liabilities	80,000	
Working capital		120,000
		420,000
Long-term liabilities		120,000
Net assets		300,000

Figure 5.3

Working capital is £120,000 in the example above.

In concrete terms, working capital consists of short-term assets and liabilities which change from day to day, even from hour to hour, in the course of business.

What do these current assets and liabilities include?

Current assets
Current assets include the following, in the order they are usually shown in a balance sheet:

1. *Stock – raw materials.* The cost of
   - raw materials used in manufacture;
   - other items not used for production, such as cleaning materials, stationery and so on.

2. *Work in progress.* The cost of work being carried out but uncompleted.
   - In a manufacturing business, it consists of materials in the process of being turned into finished goods.

    – In a construction business it represents building work in progress.

    – In a service business, it represents work being carried out, not yet completed.

3. *Stock – finished goods.*

    – In a manufacturing business, it represents manufactured goods not yet sold.

    – In a trading business, wholesale or retail, it represents goods waiting to be sold.

4. *Debtors.* Money owed to the business, such as customers who have not yet paid.

5. *Prepayments.* Expenses which are paid in advance (such as insurance, road fund licences and so on). The proportion of the charge that relates to the period after the balance sheet date is known as a prepayment.

6. *Cash at bank.* The balance held in the business's bank account.

7. *Cash in hand.* The cash at the business, either in petty cash or cash received not yet banked.

Current liabilities

Current liabilities include the following items, in the order in which they are usually shown in the balance sheet.

1. *Trade creditors.* Amounts owing to suppliers of the business for supplies of goods for manufacture or resale, goods for other expenses, or services.

2. *Other creditors.* All other amounts owing by the business, including taxes such as PAYE and VAT.

3. *Accruals.* Amounts owing, not yet billed, but which have accrued, such as telephone or electricity bills. Accruals often have to be estimated.

4. *Bank overdrafts.* Amounts owing to the bank on current account (not on loans).

5. *Loans – amounts repayable within one year.* If the amount is repayable over more than one year, then only the proportion payable within a year is included here.

6. *Other instalment loans repayable within one year.* This normally includes such things as hire purchase debts or finance lease debts. If the amount is repayable over more than one year, then only the proportion payable within a year is included here.

7. *Income in advance.* Income received in advance and therefore part of which relates to the period after the balance sheet date, such as rent received in advance.

The cyclical nature of working capital

Working capital changes from day to day. The figure shown on the balance sheet is a 'snapshot' of the working capital at that date.

> To understand the true nature of working capital, it is important to grasp the working capital cycle.

The typical manufacturing business has stocks of raw materials, which it converts into finished goods, sells to customers, then receives payment, and uses the money coming in to pay its creditors for more raw materials and other expenses.

At any time, money is circulating round the various phases of activity. Working capital shows a picture of that activity. The level of working capital should be controlled, but it may vary from time to time in response to external influences. These could include:

- seasonal changes;
- changes in fashions;
- interest rate changes;
- fluctuations in the general economic and trade cycle;
- changes in the industry-specific trade cycle;
- changes in market demand.

WHY DOES WORKING CAPITAL NEED TO BE CONTROLLED?

Cash flow – the vital element

Working capital is vital to any business.

It shows the liquidity of the business. Liquidity represents cash flow and is an important factor in the success of a business. Without good cash flow, plans are held up, and progress cannot be made. In fact, in the early stages of a new business or in the growth stage, more businesses fail because of poor liquidity than for lack of profitability.

All elements of working capital must be controlled – individually and as a whole.

STOCK CONTROL

The key stock turnover ratio seen in Chapter 2 gives a broad picture. Stock control involves more detailed measurement and control of the many different lines of stock, ensuring that obsolete or damaged stock is identified and that each stock item is at the right level.

The nature of stock

The nature of stock depends on the type of business. For example, retail businesses hold stock to sell to the public. Manufacturing and construction businesses hold stock to be made into a finished item, to be sold either to the public or to other businesses.

The level of stock as a proportion of the total assets of the business varies enormously depending on the nature of the business.

Example 5.1

A service-based business, such as an advertising agency, carries very little stock. A car dealership selling new and second-hand cars could find that the stock is the largest single item on its balance sheet.

Wholesalers

Wholesale businesses must be aware of what the public is buying and what are the latest trends. They must have the right stock at the right time to sell to retailers. Retailers will not buy out-of-date stock. Wholesalers often liqui-date stock, realising as much as possible – hence the many 'cheap' shops on the high streets, selling cheap goods bought from wholesalers because they are out of date, obsolete or otherwise unsaleable at their true price.

Retailers

Retailers must keep a constantly changing stock in front of their customers. Customers are not attracted by an unchanging display. Retailers must know whether their customers buy because the goods are cheap, or because the goods are high quality and reliable, for example.

Manufacturers

Manufacturers must constantly monitor the prices and availability of raw materials. They must keep enough stock to maintain their manufacturing process, while innovating, making new designs and finding alternative materials to use in their manufacturing process. The buyer is a key person in a manufacturing business. Providing that quality is maintained, the cost of raw materials is one of the key issues.

The cost of carrying stock

Apart from the cost of money tied up in stock being carried on the shelf, other indirect costs include the increased administrative cost of carrying stocks. Storage space is needed for stock, and the cost of space can be extremely high. Handling costs increase as the volume of stock increases. In addition, there are the possibilities of pilferage, damage and obsolescence. If excess stock is being carried, these costs and risks are correspondingly higher.

If a business carries twice as much stock as necessary, it may need extra staff to record and control the excess stock, and the risk of pilferage and obsolescence is doubled.

However, there is also a cost and danger in holding too little stock. In a manufacturing business, too little stock could mean the whole production process grinding to a halt. This could mean many production workers becoming idle, and there are further knock-on effects down the line. The 'worst case scenario' is not being able to complete production of an order and failing to meet the contract terms. The sale, and possibly the customer, is lost, and the business is left with worthless part-finished work in progress.

For a retail or wholesale business, not having adequate stock for customers is fatal. Customers will simply go elsewhere if they can get the item straightaway, rather than having to order something and wait for its arrival. Inadequate stock means a lost sale, and possibly a lost customer.

In any business, being short of stock could mean ordering a special delivery at short notice, possibly incurring extra transport costs and having to buy at a dearer price than usual.

Stock records

A reliable system of recording stock movements is essential in any business where the level of stock is material. This system should be backed up by periodic physical checks of the quantities. A stock recording system allows control of the stock levels.

In a full stock accounting system, each item of stock has its own record. The system is similar in nature to a double-entry bookkeeping system. Items coming into stock are debited and items going out are credited. A running balance shows the amount in stock at any time. This must be maintained as far as possible in real time.

Stock items are recorded in quantities, not values. These quantities may be discrete items, where they can be counted, or weights, volumes and so on for non-countable items (such as sand, cement, liquids and so on).

Many accounting software packages provide integrated stock accounting with the normal financial accounting functions.

Stock levels

If the usage of stock is constant, the level of stock could be shown as in Figure 5.4.

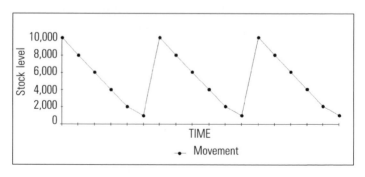

Figure 5.4 Stock levels

For each item of stock, three control levels must be determined – minimum, maximum and reorder level.

Stock holding costs are to a certain extent offset by ordering costs, which increase with the number of individual orders made. The ideal, or optimum, level of stock, is when ordering costs balance out holding costs to arrive at the lowest overall costs. This is sometimes referred to as the *economic order quantity* (EOQ).

The formula for calculating the EOQ is:

$$EOQ = \sqrt{\frac{(2 \times A \times O)}{(H)}}$$

where:

$\sqrt{}$ = square root;
A = the annual demand for the stock item;
O = the cost of placing one order;
H = the cost of holding one item of stock for one year.

However, the cost of holding one item for a year and the cost of placing one order are somewhat esoteric and not easy to arrive at. For all but the highest value items, it may not be practicable to use this formula. Further, it may produce a figure taking no account of the best terms for purchasing – such as quantity discounts, and the minimum ordering quantities.

Example 5.2

The formula gives a figure of 237 units as the EOQ, but the minimum order for the supplier is 200 units, with further orders only

▶

possible in multiples of 100. The decision then has to be made whether to order 200 or 300. If a quantity discount applies to purchases of 500 or more, the decision would also have to be made whether to take advantage of this discount.

Minimum and maximum stock levels

For each item, the minimum and maximum stock levels must be determined, recorded and controlled.

♦ The maximum quantity is determined by the quantity needed for manufacture or for resale. The aim is for enough stock to cover manufacture or sales for a normal reorder cycle. This depends on the normal quantities being used or sold and the lead-time for orders (see below). The maximum level of stock determines the amount of stock to be ordered. The present level of stock is deducted from the maximum level to arrive at the order quantity. Thus, stock must be recorded in real time. Making an order on the basis of out-of-date information can be disastrous, leading to stock levels above the maximum or below the minimum level.

♦ The minimum quantity is determined by the lead-time and the re-order level (see below), adjusted by the 'safety cushion'.

These levels should be reviewed regularly. Changing patterns of business may dictate that certain items of stock are in greater demand, or that others are in less demand, or cease to be required altogether. Changes in levels must be agreed with all involved – in a manufacturing business, the production manager, and in a retail or wholesale business, the sales manager.

Lead-time

Lead-time is the time it takes from ordering an item to its delivery into the stores. This has a bearing on the minimum level of stock and the reorder level. The lead-time should be recorded on the stock control account.

Reorder levels

The reorder level for a particular item of stock is the level at which it needs to be reordered to avoid breaching the minimum stock level.

Exercise 5.1

The XYZ Company Ltd carries 'supa-widgets'. The annual demand is 156,000 items, equally spread throughout the year. The lead-time from order to delivery is four weeks. The minimum stock level is 1,000. What should be the reorder level?

Annual usage is 156,000. Therefore weekly usage is 156,000/ 52 = 3,000 items. This lead-time is four weeks, so the reorder level should be four weeks of the usage, plus the minimum level. This works out to 13,000 items.

This can be expressed as a formula as follows:

$$(L \times U) + M$$

where:

U = usage (in weeks or days);
L = lead-time (in weeks or days);
M = minimum quantity.

The reorder level should be reviewed continuously to take account of changing circumstances. For example, a new supplier might be found who delivers the goods more quickly. If the lead-time shortens, the reorder level should be adjusted. Exercise 5.1 assumed a constant demand throughout the year. Often, demand is not evenly spread throughout the year so the reorder levels should be seasonally adjusted.

Levels of control

> Stock control can represent a significant cost and the benefits have to be weighed against the cost.

In many manufacturing businesses, there are often large numbers of different items of stock to be carried. It is also frequently the case that there are a low number of lines accounting for a high proportion of the total value of stocks. There are also large numbers of items accounting for a low proportion of the total value of stocks. In between is another category of an average number of items with an average value.

This leads to levels of stock control whereby the high value items are controlled rigorously, the middle category has a slightly lower level of control, and the high volume but low value items are subject to a much looser control. This minimises the stock control cost.

WORK IN PROGRESS CONTROL

The nature of work in progress

The nature of work in progress depends on the type of

business. Manufacturing, construction, or service-based businesses carry different types of work in progress.

In a service business, for example professional businesses, work in progress consists of the time put into the job until completion or until a billing point is reached. The invoice is raised when the job is completed. Some service businesses, such as financial advisors or estate agents, may be remunerated by commission. In such cases, the job itself must be completed before the money is earned.

In a manufacturing business, work in progress consists of the raw materials plus the amount of work that has been carried out on them until they become finished products.

In a construction business, work in progress consists of the construction itself in an incomplete state. Much money can be tied up in it.

Work in progress control

Money is tied up in work in progress. Raw materials and/ or labour have been expended on it and paid for. But it has to be progressed further before it is saleable.

Control consists in making sure that work in progress is proceeding according to its determined timetable. This is the domain of 'progress chasers', who ensure that there are no unforeseen problems holding up the work in progress.

In a service business, the most common cause of hold-ups is lack of information of some sort. This could be information from the client, or from some third party. Essential to the control of work in progress in this context is good communication with whoever is holding up the flow of information. Sometimes the person responsible has not prioritised their time adequately so that a particular job gets forgotten or left while other less important work is done. Training is essential to ensure that work is properly prioritised and progressed.

Displacement activity can also cause hold-ups. This happens when a person puts aside an important but difficult task in favour of a less important but easier one.

Example 5.3

Joanne, an accountancy clerk, occupies herself with filing and tidying the office because the next stage of the job involves contact with a known 'awkward' client who she is unwilling to face. The manager keeps chasing her to get on with the job, but she always has an excuse, and other jobs on which she is scheduled to work take precedence.

The key to unlocking this type of situation is in training. The clerk must be trained to recognise priorities and to be able to handle people – even difficult people.

Another problem is that a person who has knowledge (about the process involved or the client) may be absent – perhaps ill or on holiday – and nobody else has the required knowledge or authorisation to take up the work. Adequate training and procedures must ensure that different people can carry out the work as the need arises. In that connection, records must be adequately maintained. The information to do a particular job should be recorded and should never be just in some-body's head.

In construction or manufacturing businesses, the most common cause of delays in work in progress is lack of the right materials at the right time. The supplier has not delivered something or the item is 'out of stock'. Another cause is breakdown of machinery or equipment. There must be adequate backup.

Delays can also occur because a particular person is absent. Training must be adequate to ensure that jobs can be done by more than one person, avoiding bottlenecks. Integrated production planning seeks to ensure that the required materials are in place at the right time and that other key resources such as labour and machine time are available.

CREDITORS

Creditors represent the 'negative' part of working capital.

One way of looking at it is that the current assets represent money 'tied up', whereas the creditors represent money 'released'. Just as granting credit to customers means that a business is giving them a short-term loan, so suppliers' credit is a loan received. However, do not take this for granted and 'milk' it for all it is worth. It must be actively managed.

When first using a new supplier, agree the terms of business and of payment. A written contract is the best way to establish a new trading relationship, covering pricing, price variations, delivery, penalties, payment terms, discounts and so on. This is discussed in more detail below in the section on credit control.

The credit limit is the amount above which credit will not be allowed to extend. Any attempt to order new goods while the credit limit is exceeded will result in refusal of the supply. Some businesses are tempted to take more credit than the agreed terms, but a customer who consistently exceeds the payment terms could find themselves out of favour. Then when there is, say, a national shortage or delays with delivery, it is the late-paying customer who does not get the preferential treatment.

Larger businesses sometimes use their 'muscle' to squeeze unreasonable terms of trade and/or payment from smaller suppliers. This practice is coming under some pressure from the Better Payment Practice Group – an organisation including such bodies as the Institute of Credit Management and the British Chambers of Commerce, trying to promote better trading practices among businesses.

Good communications (both internal and external)
are important at all stages of managing supplier relationships.

For instance, proper stock control will ensure that goods are not ordered in excess of requirements and that goods are ordered in good time to avoid 'out of stock' situations. Procedures should also ensure that there is no unauthorised ordering, including a cap placed on the value of any orders without special authorisation from a director or the owner of the business.

There must be good coordination between the various departments, so that the ordering, delivery, invoicing and payment for the goods are properly sequenced. When delivery of goods is taken, there must be adequate checking procedures to ensure that the right quantity and quality is received – to tally with the supplier's delivery note and with the original order. When the invoice is received, it must be authorised, by checking against the order, the delivery, the agreed prices and the calculations. When all the authorisations have been carried out, the amount can be authorised for payment. The business's normal payment cycle must be observed, apart from any 'special payment' cases.

Discounts

Many suppliers offer discount for early settlement. To discover whether it is worth taking advantage of this, you must calculate the cost of paying early to receive the discount or take advantage of the normal payment terms.

Exercise 5.2

XYZ Ltd buys £100,000 worth of materials from ABC Ltd during a year. ABC Ltd offers 2% discount for payment within

▶

14 days of the invoice. The normal terms of payment are 60 days. XYZ Ltd's cost of finance is 14%. Calculate whether it is preferable to take the discount or utilise the normal payment terms.

To utilise the normal terms of payment gives an extra 46 days of credit. The cost of this extra credit is 2%. This can be annualised by calculating:

$$365/46 \times 2\% = 15.87\%$$

This is slightly more than the company's present cost of finance. It represents the cost of using the full payment terms. Over one year, this would cost the company £1,870 (i.e. 1.87% – the difference between the company's existing finance cost and the cost of not taking the discount). The discount option therefore appears to be better.

If there is any query or problem with the goods or services received, this must be raised with the supplier quickly. Any likely delay in payment above the normal payment terms should be discussed with the supplier(s) as quickly as possible. Early consultation can often defuse tricky situations and promote good trading relationships. In extreme circumstances, it can avoid action by disgruntled creditors for recovery by debt collectors or the courts. Good communications can help to retain future delivery of goods where these might be jeopardised.

CREDIT CONTROL

Perhaps confusingly, the control of debtors is known as credit control.

The problem

Control of stock, work in progress and creditors is within the control of the business. However, debtors are outside the business's direct control. The debtors control when they pay – indeed whether they pay at all.

Everyone is familiar with the sort of excuses heard for not paying on time. Excuses can vary from 'It's in the post', to 'The dog has swallowed the cheque book'.

Credit control differs from other controls. It is concerned with trying to achieve a pattern of behaviour by people outside the direct control of the business. Credit control therefore starts with the earliest event leading to a customer becoming a debtor.

The cost of credit

Extending credit to customers always incurs a cost. In most businesses outside retailing, credit is recognised business practice. Credit is not an option – it is a virtual necessity. The cost of extending credit to customers includes the following elements:

- *The finance cost.* When a business extends credit to customers it is giving them an interest-free short-term loan. This must be financed and the cost to the business is the rate of interest charged by the bank.

- *Opportunity cost.* Even if you do not need an overdraft from the bank, there is the lost opportunity cost. The money sitting in your customers' bank accounts could be in your own account earning interest. Another, perhaps more important, opportunity cost is that the money could have been used in some more important way inside your business – by investment in some form of business opportunity.

* *Administration cost.* The cost of administering credit control includes salaries of the staff needed (or the lost opportunity of management time involved), the stationery and postage involved, the telephone calls, and so on.

* *Bad debt cost.* The above costs are incurred for all debts. When a bad debt is written off, that is a further cost.

Monitoring debtors in total

We saw in Chapter 2 how the key ratio of days' sales outstanding is arrived at. This should be done regularly, allowing trends to be monitored.

Example 5.4

Annual sales year ended 31 December	£1,000,000	(a)
Sales ledger debts at 31 December	£14,000	(b)
Average daily sales (a/365)	£2,740	(c)
Number of days sales outstanding (b/c)	51 days	

The process can be refined further if the business includes different identifiable sectors. For example, a business could have retail sales and credit sales. If the total sales only were analysed, the real trends in credit sales could be masked by fluctuations in retail sales. Therefore the figures for the different types of business should be segregated according to the credit terms. The retail figures can be ignored for these purposes, since no period of credit is given. That will leave the credit sales analysed for a true comparison.

Example 5.5

Annual sales year ended 31 December	£1,000,000	(a)
Made up of – Retail sales	£500,000	(a1)
Credit sales	£500,000	(a2)
Sales ledger debts at 31 December	£90,000	(b)
Average daily sales (a/365)	£2,740	(c)
Made up of – Retail sales	£1,370	(c1)
Credit sales	£1,370	(c2)
Number of days credit sales outstanding (b/c2)	66 days	

If the calculation had been done using total sales, the apparent outstanding days would have been 33.

This can also be used if there are different sectors of the business with different credit terms. This might be the case, say, where export sales are involved. Thus if, for example, one sector operates on weekly credit, and another sector on monthly credit, these two sectors can be separately calculated to give the comparisons and trends for each sector individually.

Even with this refinement, however, the picture shown is only for total debtors.

Debtors' accounts must be controlled individually.
Control starts from the beginning when taking on a new customer.

Customer credit-worthiness evaluation
Basic steps must be taken before trading with another company or business. The 20/80 rule can be seen in this

context. In a large enough sample, 20% of the customers will cause 80% of the problems, complaints and bad debts. Not all problems can be foreseen or eliminated by initial screening, but a large number can be.

> Even after accepting a new customer, keep their situation under constant review. Even apparently reliable and solid customers can become bad debts.

Other customers who may have once been perceived as high risk may become less risky and more creditworthy.

Basic information
Full details of the identity of the prospective customer, such as:

◆ name of the business/company;
◆ full postal address(es);
◆ telephone number(s);
◆ fax number(s);
◆ e-mail address(es).

The structure of the business:

◆ What is the business format (limited company, partnership, limited partnership, sole trader)?

◆ Who owns the business?

◆ Regardless of the formal ownership, who is actually running the business?

- How long has the business been in existence – in its present form, or in any previous forms (e.g. a partnership may have become a limited company)?

- Are there any 'silent' or 'sleeping' partners, or other influences behind the owners/managers?

- If the business is a limited company, can the directors give any guarantees?

References

Obtain third-party verification or opinion about the prospective customer. An independent opinion is worth more than any information obtained directly from the prospective customer. All references must be authorised by the prospective customer.

- *Trade references.* Obtain references from at least two other organisations in the same trade with whom the prospective customer has done business.

- *Bank reference.* Ask direct questions, such as 'Is this customer good for credit of (say) £1,500 per month?'

- *Trade opinions.* Ask around among competitors or other businesses in the geographical area the trade association, or the local Chamber of Commerce.

- *Agency references.* Agencies such as Dun & Bradstreet or Extel can often provide information.

- *Registrar of Companies.* Permission is not necessary. The company's record at Companies House is in the public domain.

- *Financial checks.* Using the principles seen in Chapter 2, examine the prospective customer's accounts to get an idea of their financial health and look for trends. Make sure that the accounts are up to date. If companies are delinquent in filing their accounts at Companies House this could be an indication of problems.

- *Your own staff.* Staff – particularly salespeople – often have informal knowledge (either first-hand or hearsay) about other businesses. Always assess the reliability of this information before taking any action based on it.

- *A visit to the business.* A prospective customer will probably not object to a visit to their premises. Seeing things at first hand can help to gain a 'feel' for it.

When sending letters requesting references, ask as many direct questions as possible and offer to reciprocate if required. Try to find out the name of the individual to whom the request should be addressed. A stamped addressed envelope for reply is a normal courtesy. Send out all requests at the same time. Any references must be kept strictly confidential.

When looking at replies, remember that people or businesses often avoid giving an outright bad reference and will try to suggest possible problems indirectly or in code. It is always possible that the prospective customer will have selected a trade reference by making sure that that particular supplier had always been paid on time. If possible, try to have some input into selecting a trade reference at random.

A new customer is the beginning of a new trading relationship. A business-like attitude at the beginning of this relationship establishes trust. Satisfied customers are the best source of new customers.

Establishing and enforcing credit terms

Once a customer is accepted, trading terms are established. A formal contract is useful but not always possible. The degree of usefulness depends on the type of business, and the goods or services involved. Payment terms are not necessarily the first matter to be resolved or agreed.

If there is some dispute over other conditions (including delivery, quality, after-sales service and so on) then payment may well be withheld or delayed. Here are some of the matters to be settled when a new customer is accepted:

- *Price*. There should be a clearly defined method of arriving at the price of the product or service. The price must be easily understood, with no possibility of misunderstanding or different interpretation. It may be:
  - a fixed price;
  - a base price with provision for a price adjustment dependent on some outside influence (such as the cost of the raw material);
  - a price to be calculated at an agreed formula, such as the time spent on services supplied.

- *Price variation.* A clause should allow for mutually agreed or predetermined price adjustment. For instance, where the price of a service is linked to the amount of time spent on the job, the hourly or other rate may be subject to adjustment annually.

- *Delivery.* The place and date of delivery should be clearly defined. This could include such conditions as 'ex-works', 'site delivery', 'FOB', or 'CIF'. Date(s) of delivery of the goods or services are also important and should be clearly defined.

- *Penalties.* In some cases it may be necessary or normal practice to agree penalty clauses linked to delays, quality, performance or any liquidated damages.

- *Payment.* The method and timing of payment should be agreed. There are several options.

  - *Cash with order.* This can be agreed with a new customer for whom no satisfactory credit rating is obtained. No goods will be supplied and no work will be started until the payment is received and cleared through the bank.
  - *Rolling deposit.* This requires the receipt of a deposit from the customer, sufficient to cover the agreed credit limit. This deposit will always remain to the credit of the customer's account as a guarantee of future payment. Interest may or may not be paid on this deposit. This arrangement is often used until you have enough confidence in the creditworthiness of the customer.
  - *Cash before delivery.* This means agreeing a down-payment before starting any work or supplying any

goods. The down-payment should be at least enough to cover basic costs, so that the 'worst case scenario' would not leave you with a loss. The final payment must be received before the actual delivery of the goods or service.

- *Cash on delivery*. This means that the goods are paid for when delivered to the agreed address. This carries risks – of non-acceptance by the recipient and of loss or damage in transit.
- *Progress payments*. This method is common in the construction or civil engineering industry but can have application elsewhere, particularly where work to be done stretches over a long period. There are stage payments when the work has reached certain points, certified by surveyors or independent engineers. At the completion of the work the balance of the agreed price is paid. This type of work is often the subject of penalty clauses for delays.
- *Load over load (or cash next delivery)*. This relates to a specific type of delivery of goods where there is a regular weekly or monthly delivery, such as fuel deliveries to a petrol station. One delivery must be paid for before the next delivery is made.
- *Net 30 days*. This calls for payment within 30 days after the invoice date.
- *Net monthly*. This means that payment is made at the end of the month following the month in which the invoice is raised.

Credit limit
This is the amount you allow on credit to the customer.

No new orders will be executed which would cause the balance to exceed the credit limit.

The actual level is decided by reference to the perceived risk for each customer. Once established, review the credit limit regularly, and revise it to suit altered circumstances, or to reflect growing relationship and trust.

Good communication is vital. Not only must the customer know his credit limit, but your staff – particularly sales staff – must know it too.

Salespeople are always keen to get new orders – very often their salary level depends on it. Make them aware of the credit limit and the current status of the customer's account. This avoids misunderstandings and mistakes generated by overzealous salespeople. Salespeople often have a good relationship with customers, and can encourage early settlement of outstanding accounts.

Retention of title
It is common to see some sort of wording on invoices for goods, stating that the title in the goods does not pass to the buyer until payment is made. However, this has limited effectiveness. Once the goods have been delivered to the customer, they may be difficult to reclaim. They may have been operated on as part of a manufacturing process or sold on to a third party.

Written contracts
Individual trade associations and the Chartered Institute of Purchasing and Supply (tel: 01780 756777) can supply

examples of standard business terms to incorporate into contracts. However, individual terms should be written in to deal with special situations.

Accelerating billing procedures

Raise invoices as soon as possible. If goods or services have been supplied, there should be no unnecessary delay in raising and despatching the invoice.

If an invoice should have been sent at the end of April but is delayed until the beginning of May, that could cause a further month's delay in payment.

The billing procedure is not complete until it is sent to the customer. One method is to print the delivery note at the same time as the invoice. The invoice is then attached to the packaging or sent with the driver of the delivery vehicle. The customer receives the invoice at the same time as the goods. Where this is not possible, the invoice should be sent out immediately when it has been raised. If there are authorisation procedures, there should be backup in case of temporary absence of the authorising person. The price must be easily understood, with no possibility of misunderstanding or different interpretation. Use first-class post to send the invoices out.

For professional services, such as lawyers and accountants, the work involved for clients can often stretch over a long period. In these circumstances, in agreement with clients, interim invoices can be raised.

Obtaining payment

Sales ledger administration
Proper sales ledger procedures enable debts to be collected regularly and promptly. However small the business, someone must be responsible for sales ledger management and control. As the business grows, it may be possible to employ a credit controller full time.

The sales ledger shows for each customer the amounts of invoices charged, credit notes and cash received, and the amount owing to or from that customer at any time. The balances on each account are periodically listed to show the total debtors, but this list of balances does not of itself help to collect the amounts due.

Contra accounts
It sometimes happens that a customer is also a supplier with an account in the purchase ledger as well as the sales ledger. Amounts owing to you can be set off against amounts owing by you. The customer must agree the frequency of contras.

Monthly procedures
Procedures should be carried out at least monthly to control the debts. Send a statement of account to each customer, accompanied by an appropriately worded letter if any part of the debt is overdue. Beyond a certain time limit, the account should be marked for a personal letter or other form of contact, including the threat of further action to recover the money due.

When an account is overdue, it should be flagged, and no new orders accepted or work done for that customer until the account is settled. In smaller businesses, this instruction is often overridden by the owner or manager due to a special relationship with a customer.

The process of determining if part of an account is overdue is known as 'ageing', which means allocating the balance on the account according to the amount of time it has been owing. This is done by matching payments to invoices. Payments on account are allocated on a 'first in first out' basis. In practice, this procedure of ageing the debts is carried out by most computerised book keeping systems. Figure 5.5 is an example of an aged debtors list.

Name	Total	30 days	60 days	90 days+
A Aadvark	1,500.00	1,500.00		
M United	3,000.00	2,500.00	500.00	
D Trotter	2,500.00	2,250.00		250.00
Z Zeeble	500.00			500.00
Total	£7,500.00	£6,250.00	£500.00	£750.00

Figure 5.5. Aged debtors list 31 March 20xx

An aged debtors list enables delinquent accounts to be identified and efforts can be concentrated on dealing with the problem areas.

Payment methods
Many debts are still settled by cheque, although there is increasing use of debit cards, credit cards, direct debits and standing orders. Apart from retail businesses cash is rarely used.

Direct debit means that you retain control of the payment process. It is particularly useful for businesses where payment is made on regular bases, such as quarterly.

Credit card use is extremely useful for:

- retail businesses;

- businesses dealing with the general public; or

- where sales are made remotely by telephone or the Internet.

Credit cards are promoted as of benefit to customers. Advantages include:

- It allows a convenient method of payment – no matter what the hour of the day (or night).

- It is a good alternative to carrying large amounts of cash.

- It allows the customer to make a purchase if cash has run out.

- It gives the customer a method of making a purchase even when their cash flow is adverse or low.

- It facilitates unplanned or impulse buying.

- It gives access to remote purchasing – over the telephone or the Internet.

- It increases spending power – the credit limits given on credit cards are often quite generous.

It also has advantages for the selling business, including:

♦ It gives confidence that the payment is assured.

♦ It promises (and achieves) regular payment at known dates.

♦ It reduces cash handling.

♦ It can reduce administration.

♦ It provides up-to-date and regular statements of all credit card transactions.

♦ It can provide the final 'push' to persuade customers to make that purchase, especially if it is an impulse buy.

♦ It influences customers to spend more, since it has increased their spending power.

♦ It allows customers to purchase when they have no ready cash.

Against these advantages, the disadvantages must be weighed up.

♦ *Costs* – the service provider charges a transaction fee for each transaction, typically between 1% and 5%, as well as an administration fee. The decision must be made whether to pass these charges on to customers. This can be done by:
  – including the charge in general costing and mark-up policy across the board;
  – making a surcharge for credit card transactions;

    – offering a discount for cash transactions. This is, of course, done after the first process above.

♦ Although payment dates are guaranteed, the processing of these transactions takes longer than cash. If there are a large number of low-value items, this can be a distinct disadvantage.

♦ Fraud is a constant danger. If you accept a card with an obviously false signature, you can be held responsible.

♦ The danger of fraud is accentuated for sales made by telephone or over the Internet. These transactions are known as 'card not present' transactions. The credit card company may enforce an agreement that you must bear any losses due to fraud in these transactions.

♦ The procedure for becoming a merchant accepting credit cards is not automatic. Apart from the acceptance procedures, there may be some initial cost in investment in electronic equipment.

Becoming a recognised merchant

Obtaining acceptance as a merchant is done by application to a 'merchant acquirer'. These companies act as intermediaries. They authorise your transactions and ensure payment, and at the same time, pass details to the credit card companies to charge the customers' accounts.

All the main banks have merchant acquisition services. Your own bank will know your banking history and your trading pattern. However, charges vary considerably, so it is worth shopping around. Acceptance is not automatic, although it is not necessarily limited to existing businesses. New business start-ups can also obtain acceptance. However, there may be scrutiny of further factors, such as the individuals involved in the new business, and additional security may be sought. To be accepted, the merchant acquirer may vet the business, including:

- credit checks;
- recent accounts;
- trading history;
- detailed business plan;
- cash flow forecasts.

Operational costs
Once accepted, various obligations and formalities have to be set up.

- The agreement must be signed, allowing you to accept card payments.

- You will be allocated a 'merchant number' to identify your transactions.

- A 'floor limit' will have to be agreed. Above this limit, transactions must be specially authorised.

- Card-issuer logos must be displayed.

- A separate agreement must be made for 'card not present' transactions. There may be a separate merchant number for these transactions, to allow them to be identified as such. There is usually a zero floor limit for these transactions.

- Charges are agreed, depending on factors such as the card turnover, the average value of each transaction, the currencies accepted, whether the cards are credit cards or debit cards, and whether 'card not present' transactions are carried out.

- There is often an initial joining fee and the regular administration fees are usually collected by direct debit.

Internet traders are subject to additional requirements, including:

- Higher security levels are expected, including a high level of encryption and a server with virtual and physical protection.

- The computer hardware and software may be physically inspected.

- The acquirer uses a set of guidelines for this type of trading and for security of cardholders' information and details.

These requirements can be met by using a Payment Service Provider, such as Pipex Websell (www.websell.pipex.net)

Identifying valuable customers

The sales ledger can provide valuable information on identifying valuable customers – those who contribute the most to the business's profit. These customers can be given special treatment to ensure their retention and to encourage further business.

It is likely that 80% of the business's profit comes from 20% of the customers.

Many businesses have different products or services producing different levels of profit. By accurate analysis, you can identify the customers buying them. The sales ledger can also be used to identify prompt, average or slow payers.

Using these criteria, a matrix can be produced as shown in Figure 5.6. The top left box indicates the best customers – buying high-profit items, and paying promptly. The bottom right box indicates the worst customers.

Profit element of sales				
High	Average	Low		
			Prompt	
			Average	Payment history
			Slow	

Figure 5.6 Identifying valuable customers – matrix

Incentivising early payment

Despite your best efforts, customers are often delinquent in settling their accounts.

If incentives are given, customers may not need chasing to

settle the account and costs of credit control could be kept down.

Cash discounts

Discount for prompt payment is common. The invoice should show the full amount payable, with a note of the discount available and the time limit within which it is valid.

> **Example 5.5**
>
> Invoice date 13 May. Total invoice £1,000. 'Discount of 2.5% maybe deducted if payment reaches us by 27 May.'

If the net amount payable after discount is stated, some customers might pay that lower amount whether or not they comply with the time limit. They may claim this as a mistake but in fact is done deliberately. The customer should be left to work out the net payment after discount.

This discount is built into the costing structure of the goods or services. In effect, if 2.5% is offered as early settlement discount, that 2.5% is first added on to the price. If customers offer resistance, it is easy to explain that it is unfair for prompt payers to subsidise slow payers.

If customers take advantage of the discount even if not observing the time limit, their attention must be drawn to it on the first occasion. Letting it lapse is an invitation to continue doing it. The most direct method is a telephone call to point out the error and to remind them that the wrongly deducted discount will be included on the next statement. This can be reinforced on the next statement by highlighting it. If the customer persists but you do not want to risk losing them, a surcharge may be added to the invoice value. The ultimate sanction is to refuse any further business with the customer. Hard thinking is needed before retaining a customer who persists in taking unjustified discount.

The cost of cash discounts
The finance cost of offering cash discounts must be calculated.

Exercise 5.2

Your credit sales are £1 million a year. If you were to offer a 2% discount for payment within 14 days of the invoice, what would the cost be? The normal terms of payment are 60 days, which are respected by all customers at present. Your overdraft interest is 14%. Calculate whether it is preferable to offer the discount, assuming that 50% of the customers will take advantage of it. You estimate that present bad debts of £5,000 a year will halve if the discount system is offered.

Present situation:

	£	£
Credit given: 60/365 × £1,000,000 =	164,383	
Finance cost:	164,383 × 14% =	23,014
Bad debts:		5,000
Total cost:		28,114

With discount system:

	£	£
Credit given: 60/365 × £1,000,000/2 =	82,192	
Finance cost:	82,192 × 14%	11,507
Cash discount	1,000,000/2 × 2%	10,000
Bad debts		2,500
Total cost		24,007

▶

The benefit in offering the cash discount, if all the assumptions were correct, is £4,107. The credit control costs could also show savings as bad debts reduce and fewer customers take the full credit.

Issue of reminders

Another device sometimes used to incentivise early payment is to issue 'reminders for payment'. These show all the details of the goods or services supplied, but are clearly stated not to be a valid invoice for VAT purposes and that a VAT invoice will be supplied on payment. The customer is unable to reclaim the input VAT against their VAT bill until they have paid.

Making the business invaluable

If a customer is experiencing cash flow difficulties, they will often try to apply some degree of prioritisation to their creditors, paying first those creditors seen as important. One way of remaining at the head of their queue is to make your business important or invaluable to them. This may mean a high degree of excellence in quality control. Trading reputation has a positive effect on credit reputation.

Do all in your power to ensure that the quality of goods is beyond question. Keep to promises and delivery dates. Deal with queries or complaints. Sometimes it is beneficial to make some sort of compensation even when the complaint is unjustified, to enhance your reputation. Here is another fact of business life:

A customer who has had a complaint satisfactorily dealt with is more loyal than a customer who has had no complaint at all.

Delinquent debtors

Despite all efforts, there are occasions when delays occur. Identify delays quickly and deal with the causes.

Complaints and queries

Delays can occur through complaints or queries. Usually these are genuine, but they can be raised to gain more time while it is dealt with.

Therefore, make sure that there are no reasons for any complaints or queries in the invoicing procedure. Often, customers have different requirements for their own payment procedures. Try to comply with the customer's requirements. Provide as much relevant information as possible on the invoice. Items normally required include:

◆ full description of what is being invoiced;

◆ the issuing business's reference or part number and so on of the item(s) supplied;

◆ quantities, weight or measurement of the item(s) supplied;

◆ price per unit, total price and agreed quantity discount;

◆ details (if applicable) of any special pricing agreed, and by whom;

- order references from the customer;

- initials or other detail of the originating person in the customer's organisation;

- date and method of delivery of the goods;

- correct identification of the branch or department of the customer's organisation;

- if the invoice concerns services, full details of the work done, by whom and the dates concerned.

It may be useful to anticipate problems by ringing the customer a few days after the invoice has been sent to check that it has been received and that there are no queries or complaints relating to the goods or service. This is particularly useful if the customer has complained in the past. This enquiry pre-empts any complaint in the future. This approach could also be made a few days before the payment is due to ensure that payment is in the process of being authorised.

Understanding the customer's system

Depending on the size of the customer's business, there may be many processes an invoice has to go through before payment.

The invoice could be anywhere within your customer's system. A useful ploy is to make your invoices and statements brightly coloured – either of paper or printing, or to carry a prominent logo, making it immediately recognisable.

It is helpful to know the names of the people dealing with your invoices at any stage, in particular the name of the person who authorises the payment or who writes the cheque. Write these details on the customer's sales ledger account. A good personal relationship with the right person can smooth out many problems. A person known by name is less likely to fob you off with a lame excuse.

Chasing procedures
Send statements of customers' accounts regularly and on time. Customers' systems often depend on statements to settle their accounts.

Appropriate letters should be sent with statements for overdue accounts. The computer can do the donkeywork so that reliance is not placed on someone remembering to send a particular letter.

Although the wording of the letters can be standardised for particular circumstances, the actual wording should be altered from time to time. A standard letter received several times loses impact.

As an alternative to the first reminder letter, coloured stickers can be used on statements, particularly in the early stages of chasing. These stickers are cheap, bright and often humorous. Once again, repeated use deadens their impact.

Reminder letters should be brief and to the point. The point can often be made by judicious use of emboldened or highlighted sentences or phrases.

They should, of course, not constitute harassment or be in any way offensive. As with telephone manner, adopt a 'polite but firm' tone.

They should always be sent out at the right time – it is just as important not to send them too early as not to delay sending them. Warning letters should always be specific – particularly about time limits for settling the account. Finally, never make a threat you do not intend to carry out. If the final warning letter says that legal action will be taken for recovery, prepare the papers ready to go to the solicitor or debt collector.

An effective sanction is to stop any further supplies to the customer until settlement of the account. The effectiveness of this depends on the importance of your goods or services to the customer and their access to alternative suppliers. This sanction must be communicated to the customer and to your own sales staff.

When telephoning customers, all relevant details should be to hand, so that any queries can be dealt with immediately. If customers are regularly being called, a log of telephone conversations is useful so that it is known when they were last called, and who was spoken to. Be prepared for the stock replies such as 'it's in the post', and develop tactics to deal with these. If the cheque fails to arrive or it is for a different (smaller) amount, get back to the customer to rectify it.

Standard telephone techniques are quickly learnt and can pay dividends. Try to attain a 'polite but firm' attitude. Ring at different times of the day. The customer should know that you will be persistent if they do not live up to promises.

A good alternative to telephone calls is a visit to the customer, if it is geographically possible and if the amount warrants it. Personal presence is usually a good incentive to pay up.

Some small businesses use the 'one' system, reputedly with a high degree of effectiveness (see Figure 5.7).

- ♦ One invoice is sent by first-class post.
- ♦ One statement is sent at the end of the month, again by first-class post.
- ♦ One telephone call is made if the payment is three days overdue.
- ♦ One letter is sent by recorded delivery if the payment is ten days overdue.
- ♦ One visit is made by the owner of the business if the letter receives no reply within five working days.

Figure 5.7 The 'one' system.

Charging interest on overdue accounts

Since the Late Payment of Commercial Debts (Interest) Act 1998, all businesses have the right to claim interest at the official rate on overdue commercial debts.

This rate is intended to compensate for the commercial rate of interest payable on bank borrowings.

You may include a clause in the business contract for interest to be charged on outstanding debts, beyond the normal period of credit. This is known as contractual interest. It does not prejudice the business's right to charge interest under the above Act.

Getting outside help

The British Chambers of Commerce have established the Better Payment Practice Group to encourage British businesses to pay on time, and to help businesses with credit management. Their web site is www.payontime. co.uk.

Recovery of debts

When all else has failed, it becomes necessary to enforce the collection of the debt. The threat of recovery action may be enough to persuade the debtor to pay up, as long as he is persuaded that the threat will be carried out. All other avenues should be tried, and personal contact made before this final step. Take care also to ensure that there are no outstanding queries or complaints.

There are four main means of recovery.

Agencies

Many debt collection agencies operate on a 'no collection, no fee' basis. The fee is usually based on a percentage of debts recovered. Reputable agencies are registered under the Consumer Credit Act 1974 and will not engage in any underhand activities or harassment. Some agencies can also carry out overseas collections, and some may be able to trace debtors who have moved away without leaving a forwarding address.

Personal recommendation is usually a good source. A good agency should produce about a 75% success rate within one month.

Solicitors and legal proceedings
A customer receiving a letter from a solicitor will usually take it seriously and such a letter can often be effective without any further action. However, you must be willing for the solicitor to proceed with any legal action for recovery. Solicitors will usually charge on a time basis for any work done, even if it ultimately results in receiving no money. A good working relationship with the solicitor is vital for this process. Some solicitors do not undertake this work, but many will do it.

Small claims in the county court
This procedure for the recovery of small debts under £5,000 is covered in further detail below.

Filing for liquidation or bankruptcy
Bankruptcy is the process for an individual, with the alternative of an individual voluntary agreement. Liquidation, receivership and administration are the processes for limited companies.

This is a last resort, and should not be done as an idle threat, or to 'teach a lesson'. Below is a summary of bankruptcy and liquidation principles. These principles can be of practical use in credit control.

Bankruptcy and liquidation principles

It is possible to make use of the provisions of the Insolvency Act 1986. A notice may be served on a debtor company requiring the payment of the outstanding debt within three weeks. With this notice, a warning is made that any default will form the basis of a petition to wind up the company on the ground that the company is unable to pay its debts. The minimum amount of the debt for these purposes is £750. It is unwise to make this threat unless you are ready and willing to proceed with the petition.

If a business is insolvent, it is likely that all or most of its creditors will join together to instigate this. Before starting this process, weigh up the likelihood of getting any money back. When a liquidator or the official receiver is appointed, the assets of the debtor are sold – often at 'knock-down' prices – and there are official expenses of the liquidator or receiver to be deducted. After preferential debts and secured debts are paid, often not much is left for unsecured creditors. The money left from the proceeds is shared among the unsecured creditors on a pro-rata basis. If the debtor's situation is serious, there may be no money for the unsecured. Bankruptcy laws are there to provide protection for the debtor.

When bankruptcy or liquidation proceedings are started, the creditor(s) may apply to the court for an 'Examination as to Means'. This is an examination of the debtor to discover what assets and income are available. The creditor(s) must make available a reasonable sum for travelling expenses to the court to enable the debtor to attend. Failure to attend is a serious matter and the court may make an order for committal to prison.

The creditor(s) may examine the debtor at this hearing about means to pay. The debtor must produce if requested any necessary documentation to justify the answers given. This examination will provide the basis for any subsequent order for payment. Even if not taken into account directly, the information can be used to decide which method of recovery of a judgement debt is best. The debtor's evidence is given on oath.

Small claims in the county court

This procedure is a relatively simple way to recover debts under £5,000 through the county court without the use of a solicitor. Below is a step-by step guide.

Step 1

Contact your local county court to obtain form N1. You may obtain a supply of these forms to instigate future claims.

Step 2

Complete the form N1. This asks for details of the claim. Send copies also of any invoices to provide evidence. Interest may be added to the debt, either at the official rate or at any rate agreed between you and the debtor. This form also tells you to calculate and pay the fee, worked out as a percentage of the amount claimed. In working out the £5,000 limit, the interest and the fee are not taken into account.

Step 3
Send the form, with any documents, and a cheque for the court fee back to the court.

Step 4
The court will service the document, and send to you a 'Notice of Issue'. This is your receipt for the fee and gives a reference number. The debtor now becomes the defendant. The court sends a notice of the claim to the defendant at the address you have given – make sure that you have the debtor's correct current address.

Step 5
The court sends to the defendant with the notice of the claim a 'response pack' (N9). This enables the defendant to acknowledge, admit or defend the claim. This must be done within 14 days of receipt. Two days are normally given for the notice to reach the defendant before the 14 days start running.

Step 6
The defendant may react in several ways.

◆ If the defendant ignores the claim, 'judgement in default' is given to the claimant.

◆ If the defendant admits the claim and pays the claimant, the costs plus interest (if any) are also payable and are a legally enforceable debt.

- If the defendant admits the claim but asks for time to pay, this must be done on the form N9A sent with the response pack. The claimant may accept and request the judgement to be as agreed, or if he is unhappy with the request, leave the court to decide.

- If the defendant disputes or defends the claim, he must send a defence and counterclaim form (N9B) within a further 14 days. This form details the defence or counterclaim. This counterclaim need not be related to the original claim made by the claimant. Therefore ensure that the debtor has no possible grounds for a counterclaim. The defendant must also pay a court fee with this counterclaim, and if he is successful, this fee will be payable by the original claimant.

Step 7

When the counterclaim is received at the court, they will study it and issue an allocation questionnaire (N150) to all parties. Once again, this should be completed and returned within 14 days. This form enables the district judge to allocate the hearing to the right 'track'. The simplest track is 'small claims'. That is followed by 'fast' or 'multi'. The small claims track is allocated for the most straightforward claims, even with a counterclaim. This hearing is made by a district judge, the procedure is relatively informal (e.g. the judge should be addressed as 'sir' or 'madam'). The parties to the claim appear in person, or if they wish are represented by a lay person – not a barrister. The costs for this track are minimal, and there is no right of appeal except on exceptional grounds of a legal error or serious irregularity.

Step 8

The court fixes a date for the hearing with at least 21 days'
notice, and issues any special directions for the hearing
which may be considered appropriate by the district
judge. The district judge may also call all the parties to a
preliminary hearing if he considers that the special
directions need explanation, or alternatively if he
considers that the claim is ill-founded or there is no
reasonable defence.

Step 9

Each party must prepare its case for the hearing. In these
cases, the burden of proof is on the claimant. The claimant
must convince the district judge *on the balance of
probabilities* that his case is the correct one. Note the
level of proof. It is the balance of probabilities, *not* 'beyond
reasonable doubt'. The production of as much evidence as
possible will help the claimant's case. If necessary,
witnesses or expert witnesses may be called to give
evidence. Each party must also decide whether to represent
themselves or whether to appoint a legal or lay representa-
tive. Remember, though, that legal costs of representation
are not payable by the loser in this type of hearing.

Step 10

The hearing is relatively informal. The district judge will
explain the procedure he will follow and will take notes.
The hearing may also be taped. The claimant gives his side
of the case first, with any documentary evidence and
witnesses. The district judge may interrupt to clarify any
points. The defendant then puts their side of the case,
again with any documentary evidence and witnesses. Each

party may then ask the other party any questions before summing up their case. The district judge will announce his decision, with reasons, at the end of the case. This can be done immediately or after a short interval during which he considers the case. Both parties will be asked to leave the room while this happens. If the case is exceptional, the district judge may make a reserved judgement, which means that he needs more time for consideration and delivers his judgement at a later date by post. Once the judgement is given, it is legally enforceable. Appeals may only be made on grounds of a legal error or serious irregularity, and must be made within 14 days.

However, if one party was not present and not repre-sented, and if the district judge considers that there is an adequate excuse for this, application may be made to set the judgement aside. This effectively means a re-hearing.

Enforcing the judgement

Once the judgement is obtained, it must be enforced. This is the responsibility of the successful party. The mere fact that judgement has been entered is no guarantee of successful enforcement. There are several methods of enforcement of a judgement debt.

Distraint

A writ is issued and the court bailiff may distrain upon the goods of the debtor. This means seizure of the goods and sale at auction. The bailiff's fees are a prior charge on the proceeds of sale, and these types of sale often produce very small amounts – a fraction of the true market value of the goods. Therefore the claimant must be sure that the debtor has adequate goods to satisfy his claim for this type of enforcement.

Sometimes a third party, such as a spouse or hire purchase company, may claim the goods seized by the bailiff. A further problem may occur if a trustee in bankruptcy, liquidator, administrator or official receiver is appointed before the money is paid to the claimant. The proceeds must then be handed over to that person.

Charging order

A charging order may be made over any freehold or leasehold property of the debtor. This is the equivalent of a security on that property. The charging order is registered at the Land Registry, and when the property is sold, the amount of the judgement is taken as a prior claim on those proceeds. This procedure must be made through the court, and the debtor may make representation to resist the charging order. Any costs are added to the amount recoverable out of the proceeds of sale.

Garnishee order

If the debtor has a debt owing to him, the claimant may apply for a garnishee order, attaching that debt. This means that the claimant has a prior charge on that debt when it becomes due for payment. This can apply to a bank account of the debtor. The majority of garnishee orders are made on bank accounts, and once again, this can only work where the claimant is certain of the amount available in that bank account. The order must be served on the head office of the bank and at the branch where the account is held.

Attachment of earnings

If the debtor is an individual and is employed, an order may be sought to make a regular deduction from the wages of the debtor. The court will decide how much per week or month is reasonable. This method is of restricted use in enforcing debts on a sales ledger.

Equitable execution by a receiver

If the debtor has properties from which rent is due, application may be made to appoint a receiver in respect of this income. The receiver collects the rents due, and after deducting expenses, pays them over to the creditor. The receiver has to be a 'fit and proper' person, and is usually an independent solicitor or accountant.

Credit insurance

It is possible to take out insurance against credit risks.

This covers the risk of writing off bad debts but not late payment. The insurance company will carry out extensive checks on credit control procedures, and the premium will be weighted according to the insurer's view of the effectiveness of the systems. Typically, the cover is up to 90% of the credit risk of bad debts.

Writing off bad debts

Sometimes, despite all the efforts, a debt proves to be uncollectable. In these circumstances the only thing to do is to write it off. The bad debt is an expense of the business, allowable against tax and VAT.

It sometimes happens that a debt previously written off as bad is later recovered. When this happens, the amount received becomes another item of income of the business. It is taxable, and VAT becomes payable on it again.

Three golden rules for credit management
Here are three golden rules for credit management:

1. *Speed.* The longer a debt is outstanding the harder it is to collect.

2. *Consistency.* A credit policy and procedures must govern every aspect of relationships with customers, and be applied consistently and at all times. Everybody in the organisation should know and abide by the policy – especially salesmen.

3. *Accuracy.* Built-in checks can help cut down errors. Inaccuracies and errors can slow up the process of getting paid.

Appendix 1 shows a self-diagnosis health check for credit control systems, together with ten common danger signals. Any business can use these tools to improve their credit control systems.

CASH MANAGEMENT
If the ultimate goal of the control of working capital is to turn all working capital into cash, it may be asked – why is cash management important?

Firstly, a definition.

Cash in this context means money that is held either in notes and coin, or in immediately accessible funds such as a bank current account.

Every business needs a certain amount of cash. This is needed to satisfy day-to-day commitments, and to a certain extent to be in a position to exploit an opportunity when it arises. Prompt action may be needed, and ready cash is required to take advantage of the opportunity.

Cash management benefits from a couple of simple financial tools. One is cash flow forecasting, and this is considered in Chapter 9. The other is the measurement of the operating cash cycle.

Operating cash cycle

This term refers to the time period between the cash going out for materials and expenses and the cash coming in from completed sales. In a typical manufacturing business selling goods on credit, this can be represented as in Figure 5.8.

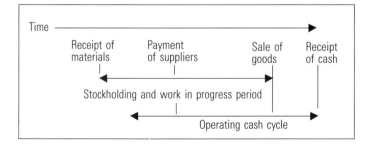

Figure 5.8 Operating cash cycle

This can also be calculated by the following formula:

$$O = R + W + F + D - C$$

where:

O = operating cash cycle
R = raw materials stock turnover days
W = work in progress days
F = finished goods stock turnover days
D = debtor days
C = creditor days.

The terms were considered in Chapter 2, apart from one minor elaboration. In Chapter 2, we dealt with stock turnover which treated stock as one global figure. In fact, stock consists of the raw materials, the work in progress and the stock of finished goods not yet sold. For these purposes, we may add those three items together to arrive at one figure for stock, then proceed as seen in Chapter 2.

6

Financial Input into Management Decisions

The financial manager has an important input into all sorts of management decisions. These impinge on selling and pricing, costing, risk management, insurance, fraud prevention, tax compliance and planning, rewarding employees, internal and financial controls, and audit.

SELLING AND PRICING

Pricing of goods or services for sale is a key management decision. Traditionally, it has been a marketing decision, and not an area in which finance managers have been greatly involved.

Sales managers will find any reason or excuse to offer a discount in order to clinch a sale. Where this is unauthorised, and particularly where it goes unchecked, the gross profit margin and the 'bottom line' suffer.

Properly used, pricing is one of many tools to achieve aims such as increasing market share or improving profitability. Pricing can, however, have far-reaching implications – the recent examples of new car prices, bank account business charges, and petrol prices have all had a great impact on companies, on public opinion and even on the government of the day.

Pricing decisions should be made on proper evidence – they should not be 'flying by the seat of your pants'.

However, sales and marketing personnel often have a gut feeling for what the market will stand, and this should be respected.

The main drivers of pricing decisions can be divided into *price factors* and *cost factors*.

There are three main price factors:

◆ Pricing according to the value to the buyer. This relies on the selling business being able to gauge the value buyers put on their products or services.

◆ Segmentation of marketplace – that is, applying different pricing policies to different segments of the market.

◆ Long-term pricing strategies. These include such things as 'penetration pricing' to enter a new market and pre-emptive pricing to retain market share. The long-term view is taken, to build a permanent market for the goods or services.

The main cost factors are:

◆ increasing volume of output to produce or improve economies of scale;

- reducing cost of production to permit greater price flexibility;

- emphasis on customer care and quality control – initially, this can increase costs, but in the long-term it should encourage increased sales;

- realistic cost allocation methods – such as activity based costing (see below). The direct and indirect costs of a particular item must be capable of accurate analysis.

COST ACCOUNTING

Cost accounting (or costing) is one type of internal reporting, concerned with the determination of costs of individual units of production or output.

As such, it is more readily adapted to and used by manufacturing businesses. However, the principles of cost accounting can be used for any business.

Determining the cost of each product is not primarily for pricing. That is a marketing decision. However, if the business knows how much each item has cost, it knows how much, if any, profit is made on its sale. It is sometimes established that a particular item cannot be sold at or above cost, and the decision must therefore be made on economic grounds whether to stop producing that item.

Costing can also be used in hypothetical situations to determine whether there is any potential to start producing and selling a new product.

One of the key concepts in costing is that of the cost centre. This is the smallest unit of production for which costs can be allocated. It may be a process or a single item or a batch of items. The correct allocation of cost centres and the accurate recording of information are the keys to meaningful costings.

Standard costing

Standard costing is a method using a cost for each unit of production under standard conditions, consisting of variable costs and an allocation of fixed costs. This standard cost is fixed in advance on the best available information at the time. When the actual figures are known, they can be compared with the standard costs. Any variances are then analysed to determine the action to be taken (if any) to rectify the situation.

Example 6.1

The standard cost of producing a batch of 10 supa-widgets is broken down as follows:

Item	Quantity	Price per unit	Amount
Rubber	2 kg	£2.50 per kg	£5.00
Steel	1.5 kg	£3 per kg	£4.50
Labour	2 hours	£7 per hour	£14.00
Factory overheads	2 hours	£6 per hour	£12.00
Fixed costs	2 hours	£4 per hour	£8.00
Total			£43.50

The actual costs have come out as follows:

Item	Quantity	Price per unit	Amount
Rubber	2.2 kg	£2.40 per kg	£5.28
Steel	1.45 kg	£2.95 per kg	£4.28
Labour	2.5 hours	£7.50 per hour	£18.75
Factory overheads	2.5 hours	£6.50 per hour	£16.25
Fixed costs	2.5 hours	£4 per hour	£10.00
Total			£54.56

Why have the costs exceeded the standard? The reason is found by analysing the variances, between price variance and volume variance. This could be done as follows (analysis of rubber variance only):

Item	Actual price per kg	Standard price per kg	Variance per kg	Standard quantity	Amount
Rubber	£2.40	£2.50	−10p	2 kg	−£0.20

Item	Actual usage kg	Standard usage kg	Variance kg	Actual price per kg	Amount
Rubber	2.2	2	+0.2	£2.40	+£0.48

This indicates that there has been a net variance of 28p. However, the variance is due to overuse of rubber, partly offset by a reduction in the cost. Similar variance analyses can be carried out on the other items, as shown in Figure 6.1.

Once variances have been established, an investigation can be made into the causes of these variances and remedial action taken. For example, the reason must be established for the variances in usage of the different raw materials.

Item	Actual price	Standard price	Variance	Standard quantity	Amount
Steel	£2.95 per kg	£3 per kg	−5p per kg	1.5 kg	−7.5p
	Actual usage	Standard usage	Variance	Actual price	Amount
	1.45 kg	1.5 kg	−0.05 kg	£2.95 per kg	−14.5p
Total variance					−22p

Item	Actual price	Standard price	Variance	Standard quantity	Amount
Labour	£7.50	£7	+50p	2 hours	+£1
	Actual usage	Standard usage	Variance	Actual price	Amount
	2.5 hours	2 hours	+0.5 hours	£7.50	+£3.75
Total variance					+£4.75

Item	Actual price	Standard price	Variance	Standard quantity	Amount
Factory over-heads	£6.50	£6	+50p	2 hours	+£1
	Actual usage	Standard usage	Variance	Actual price	Amount
	2.5 hours	2 hours	+0.5 hours	£6.50	+£3.25
Total variance					+£4.25

Item	Actual price	Standard price	Variance	Standard quantity	Amount
Fixed costs	£4	£4		2 hours	
	Actual usage	Standard usage	Variance	Actual price	Amount
	2.5 hours	2 hours	+0.5 hours	£4	+£2
Total variance					+£2

Figure 6.1 Cost variance analysis

Similarly, the reasons for the increase in cost of labour should be ascertained, and the reason for the excess time taken on the job.

Absorption costing

The basis of allocation of factory overheads and fixed costs in the above example has been the number of labour hours worked on the job. Therefore any excess time taken on the job affects the allocation of these expenses to the cost. This basis of allocation of fixed costs in proportion to the number of direct labour hours is known as absorption costing.

However, in recent years, absorption costing has been challenged. Because of greater mechanisation and auto-mation, direct labour hours are an increasingly minor cost element.

Activity based costing (abc)

This method tries to establish in greater detail what are the actual cost structures of cost centres, i.e. processes, batches, items and so on. It then allocates the fixed costs on a more appropriate basis than direct labour hours.

Example 6.2

The costs of a machine processing certain constituent parts of a product may be considered in relation to the operator's time in processing that particular patch. Thus a fairly complicated set of operations may take, say, four hours to machine a batch of 120 items. For all of this time, the operator is operating the machine. The fixed cost allocation is therefore on the basis of four hours' direct labour, or two minutes per item. A relatively simpler

▶

operation might only take, say, 15 minutes to machine a batch of 30 items. The fixed cost allocation on this basis would take account of the direct labour of a quarter of an hour, or only half a minute per item.

However, downtime is not taken into account. If the downtime for retooling and programming were half an hour in each case, this would represent only one eighth of the time on the first more complicated operation, but it doubles the time of the shorter operation. This factor would affect the allocation rates considerably, and if not accounted for could distort the true costs.

A further example relating to comparison of smaller items against larger items is the packing and transport or postage costs of sending out smaller orders compared with larger orders. If the packing and despatch department's costs are fixed and allocated to costs on the basis of direct labour hours, this could distort the true costs. Activity based costing would suggest that the department's costs be allocated as a direct cost, and the disproportionately larger amount of time spent on packing and despatching small orders would be more rationally allocated.

Throughput costing

This is another fairly recent innovation, based on the principles of activity based costing. It applies to manufacturing plants and attempts to provide relevant cost information to management by identifying bottle-necks in the production plant. A production plant or factory is a complicated network of operations, many of which cross each other and use common resources. Bottlenecks occur when several processes or components require one particular resource. If these bottlenecks can be identified, the products and processes using these resources can be prioritised by ranking the products or processes according to the contribution they make to profit. The most valuable ones are given priority.

RISK MANAGEMENT

> All business consists in taking a series of controlled risks.
> A key principle is: there is no reward without risk.

Business decisions involve weighing up potential advantages against potential risks. Risk cannot be completely avoided. The attitude to risk may vary at different stages of the business's existence and growth. Risks that may be acceptable in the initial start-up phase may not be acceptable when the business wishes to consolidate its position.

Further, as the business grows and develops, the incremental experience and resources at each stage often reduces the risk inherent in its business. The first new product launch of a business will be more risky than the fourth or fifth.

Risk does not only occur through failures. Success and growth can bring their own risks, such as overtrading. Takeovers and mergers also carry risks, particularly if the management of the acquiring company is not experienced in the business of the target company.

Financial managers may not be involved directly in all risk areas but there are many fields where they can throw light on aspects of risk management, and they should act in cooperation with other managers.

There are three basic steps in risk management:

♦ identification;
♦ assessment;
♦ management.

Identification

The following key resource areas can be liable to risk. Not all businesses are at the same degree of risk in all areas, and each business must identify its own risk areas.

♦ *Reputation, goodwill and other intangible assets.* This area is easily overlooked, but damage to goodwill can have enduring consequences. Other intangible assets such as patents or designs can be at risk through piracy.

♦ *Products and services.* These can be put at risk by poor quality control, poor cost management, inadequate selling or marketing, or pirating by competitors.

♦ *Supplies.* The availability of the right materials and services is vital for any business. These can be at risk from poor quality or late delivery.

♦ *People.* People are the most valuable resource of any business. They can be at risk from inadequate health and safety procedures, inadequate management, lack of training or poor motivation. Key employees are crucial and should be protected.

♦ *Physical assets.* These can be destroyed or damaged by fire, flood and similar incidents.

♦ *Financial assets.* These can be at risk through normal business activity. Debts can go bad, foreign transactions can suffer adverse exchange rates, investments can make a loss. Fraud is another risk area.

♦ *Administration systems.* Computer failure or virus infection can severely disrupt production and information systems. Poor design and planning, poor advice or inadequate information can also seriously affect them.

♦ *Funding.* Damage to public confidence in the business can threaten the availability of equity capital or loans. Protection of creditworthiness and the ability to provide an acceptable return on capital is of primary importance.

Sources of risk

> Once the vulnerable areas have been identified, the sources of risk must be identified.

Internal risk sources

Risk can come from within the business. Here are some of the most prominent areas:

♦ *Ineffective or non-existent management controls.* The business wanders like a ship without a rudder. Without effective management controls, a business can stray into dangerous risk areas. Financial controls are among the most important management controls.

♦ *Bad or non-existent planning.* This can lead to hold-ups in production or delivery of goods or services. The right resources must be in the right place at the right time.

♦ *Poor information.* Information is the key to organisation. If information is non-existent or inaccurate, serious risks can follow.

♦ *Poor quality control.* Poor quality products or services can threaten the entire business. In businesses that sell products, the quality of pre-sales and after-sales service should not be overlooked.

♦ *People.* People are the most valuable resource of any business. Lack of training can lead to risk. Frequent changes in the workforce mean that relatively fewer of them build up invaluable experience. However well-trained and motivated the workforce, there is the ever-present risk of accidents, disrupting the business and perhaps proving disastrous.

♦ *Industrial disputes.* Relations with the workforce are of paramount importance. Bad industrial relations disrupt business.

♦ *Machinery breakdown.* Any breakdown of machinery can seriously affect production, with consequent harm to relationships with customers awaiting orders.

- *Inherent process risk.* Some industries have inherent dangers or risks attached to the process of manufacture. The construction industry has all the hazards inherent in a building site.

- *Capital investment.* Large capital investment in equipment, property, buildings and research and development carries risks because it is dependent on stable or at least predictable market conditions and demand for a lengthy period.

External risk sources

- *Competition.* Competitors can put sales at risk by undercutting prices or offering better service. Market share is constantly the battleground of price wars. Industrial espionage is an ever-present risk. Patents, designs and technological developments could all be at risk from unprincipled competitors.

- *New entrants into the marketplace.* The barriers to new entrants differ greatly from one industry to another. In service industries, the barriers are lowest. New entrants only have to acquire the skills necessary to make an impact. Highly technological manufacturing businesses such as petrochemicals or pharmaceuticals have greater barriers.

- *Customers.* All businesses need customers but they are never entirely risk-free. There is an obvious risk in having only one customer or one main customer. In general, a larger number of customers reduces the risk element. Customers also bring the risk of defaulting on their debts.

- *Markets.* Nothing is static and markets constantly change. Inadequate market research can undermine the whole basis of new product or service launches. Concentration of business output in one or two markets can leave the business vulnerable to changes in demand.

- *Suppliers.* Spread your risks. Having too few suppliers leaves you at risk of being unable to obtain vital supplies of materials. The relative strengths of supplier and customer are also relevant. A small business does not have much 'clout' with a large supplier concern. If the supplier ceased production of the items, are there alternative suppliers?

- *Crime.* Fraud is an ever present and growing threat in a highly technological age. Other forms of crime still pose risks. Crime can be committed by disaffected employees or by complete outsiders who have identified areas (such as large quantities of cash) that can be targeted.

- *The economy.* The national and international economy affects businesses. Interest rates, inflation, deflation, recessions, exchange rates – these are all part of the economic cycles affecting markets and operations.

- *Government legislation.* Policies of successive governments, such as the minimum wage, can affect businesses. Taxation policies change – usually annually. Trading overseas puts you at risk of influence from foreign governments. Politically or economically unstable countries increase the risk.

◆ *Demographic issues*. Changes in population profiles affect businesses by altering the structure of markets or the availability of labour for the workforce.

◆ *Social issues*. Changes in public opinion on matters such as tobacco, alcohol and 'green' issues can affect markets. Environmental issues are particularly relevant, as the public and other interest groups become readier to sue businesses for environmental damage.

◆ *Natural phenomena*. Weather conditions, flood, drought and earthquake can have an obvious primary and secondary effect on businesses. Diseases of humans and of animals can also have their effect. Often the most pressing concern in these cases is the 'clear-up' operation, and getting back to normal working as soon as possible.

Assessment

Many potential areas of risk can seem overwhelming. However, not all risk areas are equally serious, and they must be assessed.

Assessing the risk factor means trying to measure the likelihood of the risk occurring and the impact if it should occur. Remember the principle: if you can't measure, it you can't control it.

When risk is assessed, you can decide where to target resources.

Likelihood

Some risks are uncertain by their nature, such as industrial accidents or human or animal disease. When events are part of a natural or economic cycle, and when the population is large enough, those risks can be susceptible to statistical probability analysis.

Some risk areas can be foreseen, if not predicted with certainty, by a combination of experience and management intuition. Experience can be shared through trade associations, chambers of commerce and so on. Businesses are keen to share this sort of knowledge. It helps protect their industry and gives no individual business a competitive edge. You can also generate your own information bank for specific risk areas – such as keeping accurate records of accidents, monitoring customer complaints, keeping a log of machinery breakdowns, and so on.

Potential impact

The direct effect of the occurrence of a risk can usually be measured in financial terms. This can include

- the cost of replacement of the lost or damaged resource;
- the lost opportunity costs; and
- downtime costs.

The indirect effects are more difficult to measure or quantify. Things like the knock-on effect of a failure of an activity in one department may be felt in other departments. The more distant from the original event, the more difficult is measurement. Effects like the ultimate impact on the business's reputation may be potential rather than realised.

Assessment
The final assessment of risk depends on the interplay between the likelihood and the impact of a risk.

♦ A low likelihood and low impact event will not cause much concern. Action may not be cost effective.

♦ A high likelihood but low impact event causes more concern, but will be relegated on the action plan until higher-profile events have been dealt with. Any action proposed must be subjected to assessment of its cost effectiveness.

♦ Low likelihood but high impact events are the most insidious – they may creep up unnoticed and suddenly explode with lethal consequences. For example, if a drug developed by a pharmaceutical company was shown to have damaging side effects, the potential impact could be fatal for the company. These risks must be acted upon, but not necessarily as the first priority.

♦ High likelihood and high impact events – such as a fire or explosion at a fireworks factory – demand the most urgent action. They must be acted upon with the highest priority.

A matrix such as in Figure 6.2 helps decision-making.

High likelihood Low impact	High likelihood High impact
Low likelihood Low impact	Low likelihood High impact

Figure 6.2. Decision-making risk matrix

The lowest concern would be in the bottom left corner, and the highest in the top right corner. The boundaries between the different corners are not sharp, but they merge into each other, and judgements must be made as to which are the most important. Each case must be considered on its own merits.

Management of risk

Once risk has been identified and assessed, action must be taken.

Agreed policies must be in place, like the limits of acceptable and unacceptable risks, the structure of decision-making, and the limits of authority of each level of management.

Attitudes to risk change as the business develops, so risk management policy must be constantly reviewed. Once agreed, changes must be communicated effectively to all levels of management, and their responsibilities for risk identification and assessment agreed with them.

Reducing the likelihood and potential impact of the event controls risk. Remember: prevention is better than cure.

Minimisation of likelihood

Several steps can be taken to minimise the likelihood of the event.

- *Specialist knowledge and experience.* For example, handling and transporting hazardous goods could be subcontracted to a specialist haulage firm.

- *Don't put all your eggs in one basket.* This applies to customers, suppliers and key staff. For instance, too great a reliance on one or a few customers or seasonal sales could be rectified by a greater emphasis on developing new markets and reducing the seasonal nature of the trade.

- *Develop information systems to warn of recognised or potential risks.* Monitoring the situation is a continuous process. Once an event is identified there must be procedures to report the occurrence to the right person.

- *Make physical alterations or improvements to premises*, such as fire precautions, closed circuit cameras or electronic surveillance equipment. Security systems are not always expensive. The local police crime prevention unit can often advise on systems, some of which can be linked to police response units. Insurance companies can also provide advice.

- *Training of all staff* on general risk issues, and specific training for staff in particular areas – such as credit control for sales ledger clerks. Employee awareness of risk is vital to reduce the likelihood of an event.

Minimisation of impact

◆ *Insurance*. This is an important part of your action plan for risks and is dealt with in more detail below.

◆ *Contingency planning*. Plans should be on hand, and regularly reviewed to put into place if an adverse event takes place. This can help you get back to normal running as soon as possible. Plans should include a detailed timetable for instigating backup procedures.

Risk management is treated in more detail in *Risk Management Standard* published jointly by the Institute of Risk Management, the Association of Insurance and Risk Managers and the National Forum for Risk Management in the Public Sector (2002).

INSURING AGAINST RISKS

The principle of insurance is that of pooled risk. Many individuals and businesses pay into a pool operated by an insurance company, and those few that suffer the insured risk get financial compensation. In practical terms, insurance is one of those recurring expenses and it is tempting to ask if you could miss it out. You seem to pay in and never make a claim.

> Do not ask 'can I afford to pay it?'
> — ask instead 'can I afford not to pay it?'

Some insurances are compulsory.

- If you have employees, you are obliged to display an employer's liability insurance certificate.

- Certain types of business may be required to have particular types of cover under health, fire and safety regulations.

- Every road vehicle must carry at least third-party insurance cover.

- If a business has a mortgage on property, the mortgagor will almost certainly require at least fire and damage insurance cover on the building.

Reviewing insurance

Insurances must always be kept under review. It is probably not a good idea to change insurance companies every year, chasing after the cheapest premiums. But it usually pays to have a thorough insurance review every few years.

Disclosure

Contracts of insurance are of 'utmost good faith'. That means that all relevant facts must be disclosed to the insurer. Failure to do this could invalidate the policy. It is easy to overlook changes which could materially affect the risk taken on by the insurer, such as:

- a new product line;
- a new overseas market for exports;
- a change in the tenancy of buildings, or the way in which buildings are occupied;
- a change in the numbers of the workforce.

All these could be material facts to be disclosed. A regular review should ensure that these items are not overlooked.

The insurance industry is very sophisticated and cover is available for every risk imaginable. However, do not be talked into taking out every new insurance product that comes along.

Level of cover

An occasional review should focus on making sure the right level of cover is in force.

> The level of cover is extremely important.
> Underinsurance can be almost as devastating as no insurance.

Sometimes, the level of cover set some years ago is now excessive. The level of cover is particularly important in the following types of insurance:

- *Buildings* – the rebuilding cost should be insured, not the market value.

- *Stock* – the cover should be for the maximum amount of stock carried at any one time.

- *Business interruption* – usual cover is for 18 months' loss of profits based on the last annual profit figure.

- *Equipment and machinery* – cover should be for the cost of replacing machinery, not necessarily its original cost.

Premiums

An insurance broker can survey the market to check whether better premiums are available. Bear the following in mind:

◆ *Uninsured excess* – if you can accept a slightly higher level of excess, the premium is reduced.

◆ *Discounts* – insurance companies often offer discounts if you can show that you have taken precautionary measures to reduce risk (for example by fitting alarms or fire extinguisher sprinkling systems). Many insurers write warranties into their policies requiring at least some risk management procedures in place.

◆ *Frequency of premium* – it may be possible to pay the premium quarterly or monthly instead of annually.

◆ *Long-term agreements* – lower premiums or fixed rates may be obtained by agreeing a longer-term contract with the insurance company – say, for three years.

FRAUD PREVENTION

Fraud is another area of risk management, but it is a major crime area and is usually on the increase during a period of economic downturn or recession.

A key area of financial management is fraud prevention and the old adage remains true: prevention is better than cure.

Fraud can occur at any level – from an employee trying to defraud the employer to a business trying to defraud other parties, including the Inland Revenue and Customs and Excise, or insurance companies by bogus insurance claims. Fraud may also be aimed at investors, creditors or banks.

Shareholders in private companies can be the target of fraud. If the structure of a private company is such that a minority shareholder – or even a 50% shareholder – is not involved in the day-to-day running of the company, the other owners can try to defraud the minority shareholder of value. This could arise, for example, by exceeding the normal limits for exercising prudence in preparing company accounts or making excessive provisions against assets such as work in progress or debtors to depress profits and justify a lower share valuation.

Then there are always scams by which unscrupulous operators try to extract money from businesses.

Example 6.1

One scam in recent years involved the use of bogus invoices, purporting to come from directories or registers. These bogus invoices, if not subject to control procedures, would often be paid without further inquiry and the bogus operator would quickly move on to another address. Proper authorisation procedures should uncover this fraud.

Fraudsters will often try to capitalise on two factors – lack of time and materiality. Many businesses – particularly smaller ones – do not have the time or procedures to deal with much detailed paperwork. If the scam is kept to a reasonable cash figure, it may well pass unnoticed. Any amount below, say, £100 may be passed without further enquiry.

Example 6.2

A service contract for maintenance of machinery or equipment may specify that up to two routine service visits are included in the annual fee, with only exceptional visits or major repairs charged separately. However, the service company actually invoices for the routine maintenance visit. The checking procedure on the invoice established that the visit was actually made, and the invoice is passed for payment – but nobody has checked against the original contract. If this point is picked up, the service company apologies for this 'error' and cancels the invoice.

Further examples include:

◆ unwarranted use of direct debit instructions – control over the payment is exercised by the supplier and unauthorised increases in amounts collected in this way or dates of collection could go unnoticed by the payer;

◆ unnecessarily complicated invoicing which discourages any attempt at clarifying exactly what is being charged for.

However, many fraudsters succumb to greed. What could remain undetected if kept at a lower level becomes their downfall. For example, small amounts of goods pilfered from stock can go unnoticed for a long time – particularly if stock control procedures are lax. However, if the practice is escalated, the amounts involved excite attention and the pilferage is discovered.

Cash fraud

Where the business handles cash – as in retail trading – the opportunities for fraud are always present. An employee stealing cash can perpetrate this on the business, or fraud can be perpetrated on the Inland Revenue by concealing cash transactions and evading tax.

Cash fraud is easier where there is a large number of transactions for relatively small amounts. It is a constant concern for banking businesses and building societies, whose main business includes handling cash.

Controls should be in place where cash handling is a significant part of the business. These can include:

♦ moving staff handling cash to different locations without notice;
♦ carrying out spot checks without notice; and
♦ ensuring that all staff take their holidays. Failure of staff to take holidays is often a pointer to fraud.

In general, controls should ensure that in order to carry out fraud there would have to be collusion between at least two people.

Employee fraud

One particular fraud occurs in wages departments and is known as 'ghosting'. This involves setting up employee records for fictitious people and collecting the extra wages paid. These wages can be paid either in cash, which is preferable to the perpetrator, or by diversion to a bank account. The bank account, however, always leaves a trail that can be uncovered at a later time.

Regular spot checks ensure that all employees actually exist.

Technology fraud

Major areas of fraud occur in technology and the Internet. A serious area of concern is the diversion of credit card details allowing fraudsters to use bogus credit card numbers to obtain goods or services from the Internet or over the telephone.

Bogus businesses can also be set up online, taking orders and accepting payment only by cheque or postal order. They accept the cash without delivering goods, and quickly move on to a new bogus identity at a new website. This type of fraud is basically the same as the bogus invoice type seen earlier. Assured identification of any supplier to whom payment is made is vital. Some fraudsters attempt to make their website resemble that of a well-known business or brand, and thereby attract payments for non-existent goods or services. Websites can conceal foreign addresses, so it is important that the website address is 'backed up' by a real, bricks-and-mortar address (not just a postbox address).

Data protection

Ensuring the security and safety of data is a major concern. Business data can be sensitive and leakage could be detrimental to you.

When data is not stored in a physical form but in electronic form, fraudsters can access it electronically.

Data stored electronically can also be lost. The loss of information incurs time in reconstructing the data.

Access to data should be controlled and adequate backup taken. Often, however, these two criteria adversely affect each other. Password protection and encryption can control access. Backup copies should be kept physically separate from the original data. Computers with sensitive information can be separated from the network and not connected to the Internet to reduce vulnerability.

The Data Protection Act 1998 provides a legal framework for the protection of data and businesses holding certain types of data must register under this Act. Those businesses must specify how their data is protected and allow individuals access to information held about themselves. This gives rise to problems of identification of those individuals wishing to access their information.

Reporting fraud
If a fraud is discovered, there are good reasons to report it to the police authorities, not the least being the deterrent effect. However, the process of reporting and investigation

by the police involves considerable disruption to the normal business routine. The police need original documentation, which provides them with 'best evidence'. They can, of course, provide copies or photographs of any item they retain, but it can still seriously disrupt.

As is common, many cases of fraud involve computer records and the police are required to seize the computerised storage medium. Again, the police can make images or copies of data, but this is also a disruptive process.

Creating an anti-fraud culture

Steps can be taken to prevent fraud by encouraging an anti-fraud culture.

This can include publishing an anti-fraud policy and other measures. The policy document could include some or all of the following items:

◆ What the business will do if fraud is suspected.
◆ What the employees should do if they suspect fraud.
◆ Training facilities for recognising fraud.
◆ The procedure for assessing fraud risk.
◆ IT controls should be kept strictly confidential to the IT department.
◆ Internal controls should be appropriate to the assessed risks.
◆ Actively instigate anti-fraud investigations.

Signs of weakness in systems

It is always useful to be aware of signs of weakness and by regular monitoring to eradicate them. Some signs of weakness are:

◆ Staff not taking holidays.

◆ Staff working abnormal or unusually long hours.

◆ Paying staff less than the industry norm.

◆ Lack of separation of duties, particularly where handling cash is involved.

◆ Branches in remote locations not being reviewed as regularly or as rigorously as other branches.

◆ Unexplained variances from budget – either favourable or unfavourable.

◆ Clusters of transactions just below the authorisation limit.

TAX COMPLIANCE AND PLANNING

Taxation is a major area of finance affecting virtually every business and other organisation.

Taxes are direct or indirect. *Direct taxes* are those levied on income (such as Income Tax and Corporation Tax). *Indirect taxes* are those levied on spending (such as Value Added Tax and Excise Duties).

My book *Small Business Tax Guide* (How to Books) gives an insight into compliance and planning for the many taxes affecting small businesses.

REWARDING EMPLOYEES

Rewards generally
Rewarding employees involves setting fair rates of pay and deciding whether any extra benefits should be paid. Any bonus schemes should be easily understood and seen to be fair. Perhaps the most problematic area is that of directors' remuneration. However, other employees seen as key employees may also be the subjects of special packages to retain their services. Details of employee rewards and incentives, including share schemes, are given in my book *Small Business Tax Guide* (How To Books).

INTERNAL AND FINANCIAL CONTROLS
Internal controls have several aims:

- ensuring adherence to management decisions and policies;
- reducing the risk of error;
- reducing the risk of theft or fraud;
- safeguarding assets;
- ensuring the accuracy and completeness of the financial and other records.

Non-financial controls
Not all controls are financial in nature. In certain businesses, control and security of the physical assets is extremely important, particularly where the assets are of high value and are relatively portable.

Another important matter is physical access to the premises. Thus key distribution is relevant, and control should be kept over the personnel authorised to gain access to the premises. Leavers should of course hand in their keys.

Information technology

The following controls are appropriate:

♦ Regular backups of all data should be made and stored in a separate location.

♦ Stand-by equipment should be available in the case of mechanical failure.

♦ Physical access to areas holding sensitive information should be controlled, perhaps by sign-in systems or visitors' and staff badges.

♦ Password protection should be enabled and the passwords changed regularly.

♦ Logging-off procedures should be enforced when leaving terminals at any time, such as lunch breaks.

♦ Passwords should not be left visible near the computers.

♦ Unauthorised computers, especially laptops, should not be brought into the computer areas.

♦ Access to the Internet should be strictly controlled. Adequate physical and software protection should also be in place against viruses and other destructive devices.

Financial controls

Apart from cash (which usually forms only a relatively minor proportion of the total financial assets), the financial assets of a business are in an intangible form and therefore susceptible to fraud.

Internal controls should be recorded and subject to regular review. Compliance with internal controls should be regularly monitored.

Integral to the internal control system is the competence of staff at all levels to carry out their duties. Regular checks should be carried out that all staff are competent and qualified for their activities. Training should be monitored and instituted where necessary.

Stock control

The nature of the business will dictate the level and type of stock held, and therefore the nature of stock controls. Stock can include:

- raw materials;
- work in progress;
- components;
- finished goods;
- consumable stores; and
- office supplies.

Some of the main controls are as follows:

- a written system for receiving, checking and reordering goods for stock;

- a named person responsible for the physical security of stocks, and precautions against theft, deterioration or misuse;

- if possible, those responsible for keeping stock records should not have direct physical access to stocks;

- minimum, maximum and reorder levels should be recorded for each item of stock, and regularly reviewed;

- regular reconciliations of stock records with the financial accounting records;

- a system for recording issues of goods out of stores to production;

- adequate records for any stock in the hands of third parties;

- a named person responsible for carrying out regular physical stock checks;

- a recognised policy of authorised entry to the stores – unauthorised entry should not be permitted;

- regular review of stock for damage, deterioration or obsolescence;

- scrap and waste sales recorded, and proceeds accounted for.

Ordering, purchase invoice authorisation and checking

Proper authorisation procedures must be in place for all incoming invoices, to discover and eliminate unauthorised or fraudulent invoicing.

The *ordering of goods* should be subject to the following controls:

- Requisitions from stores for replacement items should be within the stock control levels and reorder quantities.

- Orders placed should be authorised, including procedures to ensure that competitive quotes are obtained where appropriate.

- Purchase order forms should be kept secure and the responsibility of a named person.

Incoming invoices should be checked and authorised for the following:

- *Authorisation and confirmation of order.* All invoices should quote an order number or reference. The person responsible for making the order should verify the amount, quality and agreed price of the order against the invoice.

- *Arithmetical accuracy.* A simple arithmetical check can eliminate errors. The supplier must correct and reissue erroneous invoices.

♦ *Actual receipt of the goods or services.* In the case of goods, a delivery note should confirm the actual date and quantity of goods received, to be verified against the invoice. In the case of services, the department receiving the services should authorise the invoice. There should be regular reconciliations of goods received against goods ordered.

♦ *Payment terms.* Most invoices will be subject to normal payment terms. In this case, they will go through the payment run on the purchase ledger at the normal dates. Special payment terms must be flagged so that payment is made at the proper date.

A simple rubber stamp is often used on the invoice, and when initialled in all relevant places the invoice is correctly authorised. Figure 6.3 shows an example.

	Authorised by:
Order placed – number	
Arithmetical accuracy	
Goods received delivery note no.	
Special payment terms	

Figure 6.3. Example of authorisation stamp for incoming invoices

Only when incoming invoices have been checked and authorised, should they be entered in the purchases ledger. Once the invoice has been entered in the purchases ledger, it can be considered as verified.

Sales and debtors

This side of the administration presents many of the same features as the purchases side. However, some other features are as follows:

- Checks should be made on customer orders, to ensure that they are followed through to requisitions of stock, despatch of the goods and invoicing.

- The pricing of goods on invoices should be supervised.

- Discounts offered, special pricing, 'free of charge' goods and exchanges of goods should be supervised.

- A named person should have responsibility over blank invoice and credit note stationery.

- An independent person should check all goods leaving the premises and authorisation of despatches.

- There should be reconciliations made of goods ordered goods despatched, and goods invoiced to customers.

- Sales ledger procedures should be regularly adhered to and subject to review.

- All statements of account should be sent immediately to customers. No statements should be altered.

- Credit notes should be authorised by a named person.

- A named person should be responsible for authorisation of bad debts written off. The reason for any bad debts should be verifiable on file.

Separation of duties

A key element of internal control is to ensure that, as far as possible, no one employee has control of all aspects of a transaction.

Tasks are divided so that no one person carries out all of them. The opportunity of manipulating the system is thereby greatly reduced as any attempt at fraud requires collusion by at least two people.

In the sales department, there are several different operations:

- receiving an order from a customer;
- requisitioning the item from stock or special manufacture;
- delivery of the goods or services;
- invoicing;
- sales ledger procedures.

Even at the receipt of money, there are several stages:

- the actual receipt of the cash or cheque;
- recording it in a paying in book;
- paying it in to the bank.

All of these processes should be separated as far as possible within the staffing levels.

Payment by direct debit, standing order or electronic funds transfer alleviates some of these security concerns.

Staffing matters

Internal controls related to staff include the following:

♦ Are loans to employees authorised? If so, who takes advantage of them and are any repayments overdue?

♦ Does the company offer any preferential rates or discounts for staff? Are these being abused?

♦ Do any staff not take their holidays?

♦ Do any staff regularly work abnormally long overtime, particularly if other staff do not do so?

Cash controls

Where cash is involved in any business, the opportunities for fraud or theft are much greater.

Investigation and regular checks can uncover anomalies such as unnecessary delays between receiving cash and depositing it in the bank.

Cash controls include the following:

♦ Two people should be present when cashing up or reconciling cash balances.

- All cash receipts should be banked intact, with no deductions for small cash payments.

- Opening the post each day should be done by at least two people, to ensure that any incoming money is not stolen at this point.

- Lists should be kept of all money received in the post to compare with actual bankings on a random spot check basis.

- Petty cash payments should be made from a petty cash account, under the control of a different person who handles the other cash in the business.

- Petty cash should be drawn separately from the bank account and accounted for before any further petty cash is drawn to replenish the petty cash balance.

Authorisation levels

A system should be in place to ensure that proper authorisation is applied to transactions at all levels. For instance, an administrative secretary could be authorised to order office stationery up to a value of, say, £50. Expenditure on a capital project of several hundreds of thousands could require the authorisation of the board and cheque signature requirements of at least two specifically authorised people.

Cheque signatures

- At a certain level cheques should carry at least two signatures – which could be any two signatures from the list of authorised signatures.

- Higher values of transaction could specify the actual signatories required.

- Blank cheques should not be pre-signed by anyone.

- Stamping or printing machines for cheque signature present their own particular and obvious problems of security. The physical security of the machine should be of the highest priority.

- Preparation of cheques should be in the hands of a non-authorised person.

- Once cheques have been signed, they should be despatched without delay.

Wages

The following are some wages controls:

- Employees should have written contracts.

- A named person should have authority for hiring and firing.

- A named person should authorise changes to rates of pay.

- A named person should authorise overtime carried out.

- A named person should authorise advances or loans against wages and control their recovery.

- The system of recording hours worked, piecework and calculation of wages should be strictly adhered to.

- Special procedures should be in place for dealing with absences and short notice departures.

- Wages should be paid to employees' bank accounts, except where cash wages are unavoidable, and authorised.

- Payment of cash wages should be supervised by a named, authorised person.

- The identity of those collecting cash wages should be verified.

- Uncollected cash wages should be the subject of specific security procedures.

Fixed assets

The following controls should be in place:

- A named person should authorise capital expenditure.

- A named person should authorise the sale or scrapping of fixed assets.

- Receipts from the disposal of fixed assets should be accounted for.

- A named person should be responsible for maintaining a full register of fixed assets, including their location.

- A written policy must exist on the distinction between capital expenditure and revenue expenditure.

- The register(s) of fixed assets must be reconciled regularly with a physical check of the assets, and the financial accounts.

- A named person should keep the maintenance and repair log of all assets.

- There should be a written policy on the depreciation rates of all fixed assets.

Investments

The following controls should be maintained:

- A named person should authorise the purchase of investments.

- A different person to the one authorising purchase should ensure custody of the title documents.

- Physical security of title documents must be ensured – in a locked, fireproof safe or cabinet.

- A detailed investment register should be kept and reconciled regularly to the physical check of title documents.

- Stockbrokers' notes on the purchase or sale of investments should be reconciled to the title documents held and the register. Calculations of stockbrokers' charges should be checked.

- Income from investments, including dividends, interest and bonus issues, should be reconciled to the financial accounts.

AUDIT

Audit is a key area of control in business finance.

Companies of a certain size are obliged to have an external audit and many large companies have internal audit departments.

External audit

External audit involves an independent person or firm (usually chartered or certified accountants) making examinations to enable them to certify that the financial statements give a true and fair view of the company's transactions in the accounting period and of the state of the company's affairs at the balance sheet date. These examinations include random checking of entries in the accounting records against verifying documentation, statistical analysis of figures, verifying valuations used in the financial statements and thorough examination of matters of principle.

External auditors are appointed by and report to the members of the company – that is, the shareholders. However, other third parties may place reliance on the auditor's report, including:

- Inland Revenue and Customs and Excise;
- banks and other lenders;
- prospective purchasers of the business in a takeover;
- suppliers to the company wishing to establish credit terms;
- customers of the company.

Since such importance is attached to the auditor's report, it is useful to know what the report is likely to say. Auditors' reports are of two basic kinds:

1. *Unqualified*, sometimes also referred to as a 'clean' report. This means that the auditor is satisfied that the company's financial statements give a true and fair view. In itself, this is not a guarantee that there are no errors in the financial statements, but it gives readers a high degree of assurance in the integrity of the accounts.

2. *Qualified.* This indicates a reservation the auditor may have on some aspect of the financial statements. The qualification may be relatively minor, but the wording of any qualified report should be examined carefully. For example, a qualified report may say that the financial statements give a true and fair view 'subject to ...', followed by the areas of reservation. This may be something like a deviation from a published Financial Reporting Standard. The auditor will comment on this, and whether the deviation is appropriate to the company's business.

   Other qualifications may be more serious, arising from the auditor's disagreement with the way particular items have been treated. These qualifications are likely to be signalled in the auditor's report by saying that the financial statements give a true and fair view 'except for ...' followed by the matter of disagreement. This could arise if, for example, the auditor believed that a larger provision should be made for debts likely to prove irrecoverable.

   A fundamental disagreement would lead the report to say that, in the auditor's opinion, the financial statements *do not* give a true and fair view. In this case, the auditor would have to explain the basis for this opinion and the matters that led him to issue this negative report.

The consequences of a qualified report depend on the exact nature of the qualification. A relatively minor qualification may not cause too many ripples. However, a serious qualification would first of all cause concern to the shareholders. The auditor's report is their assurance that their company is being run well on their behalf by the directors and managers.

A serious qualification could lead to a fall in the value of the company's shares, and therefore be of major concern to the shareholders. This in turn could lead to calls for the removal of some or all of the directors or managers.

It is vitally important that financial managers do all in their power to ensure that an auditor's report is unqualified.

The management of the business itself may also find certain aspects of the audit useful, for example:

◆ The audit can provide a further 'line of defence' against fraud and error.

◆ The audit can bring to light weaknesses in the internal controls of the company or in its accounting systems.

◆ The auditors can help suggest further ways to control the business.

Auditors require unfettered access to the company's records. You must ensure that all the company's records are kept in a readily understandable form and that all necessary documentation, including invoices, contracts and so on, is kept systematically filed. You must be sufficiently aware of the business's finances to discuss relevant matters with the auditor. The audit represents a significant expense and the cost can be kept down as far as possible by making the audit easier. Do not simply react to requests from the auditor, but be proactive in helping. Below are some items which could well be on the agenda of meetings between the financial management and the auditor:

◆ any problems perceived since the last audit;
◆ a thorough review of the internal control systems;
◆ a review of the company's accounting policies;
◆ discussion of the materiality level;
◆ a review of the company's present circumstances, and finances;
◆ valuations of important assets;
◆ a review of any contingent liabilities;
◆ authorisations to third parties to give information directly to the auditor;
◆ details of transactions with directors;
◆ a review of capital raised during the accounting period;
◆ a timetable for the audit;
◆ possible areas of doubt which could result in a qualified audit report.

7

Measures of Success

In this chapter we look at different measures used to judge success or failure.

First, we look at the approach an outsider might use to decide whether to invest his money in a business. We consider an alternative to traditional methods, the 'total shareholder value' approach. Then we look at four key measures of success before looking at other, non-financial corporate values.

Finally, we look at the appraisal of future projects, including the analysis of the risk element.

THE INVESTMENT APPROACH

This involves looking at your business from an external viewpoint.

What would a shrewd investor look for before investing money in your business? If you have what they look for, you have achieved a measure of success.

Investment criteria

People invest their money in businesses for a variety of reasons. Some want maximum income immediately. Some may look for an income that has a reasonable chance of increasing from year to year. Others look for capital growth, and yet others may look for a balance of income and growth.

Investment terms

In order to understand the various terms used in investment (and in particular the terms involved in investing in companies), read through Appendix 2 now.

Investment decisions

The risk/reward equation is central to investment decisions. If you seek to minimise risk you will look for shares with preferential rights, debentures or other secured loan stocks. Those willing to take greater risk in return for greater rewards will accept ordinary shares and unsecured loan stocks.

Investors with sufficient money to invest seek to spread their risks as far as possible. Their investment portfolio is likely to include investments in different market sectors and with varying risk profiles.

TOTAL SHAREHOLDER VALUE

You may feel that the performance shown by the bottom line of the profit and loss account and the balance sheet does not give a full picture of the value of your stake in the business.

> Total shareholder value is an approach looking at the totality of what owners receive in return for their investment of capital – and of time – in the business.

Thus it includes dividends paid, capital gains, the expectation of future profits and, if the owner works, the salary received. It could also take into account intangibles such as the status achieved and perhaps other benefits in kind rather than in money.

Traditional measures

Traditional accounting figures such as the profit and loss account and balance sheet measure past performance and therefore do not give any value or credit for future prospects. Certain accounting conventions also mean that the traditional figures do not give full significance to the true value. These conventions include the following:

- *Historic costs*. Although limited revaluations are allowed, such as for land and buildings, traditional balance sheets are generally based on historic costs less depreciation. These may not reflect true current values.

- *The accruals principle*. This means that costs and revenues are matched in an accounting period. Cash flow is ignored. Cash flow statements, when added to accounts, greatly assist the appraisal of the value of a business.

Investment valuation. Prudence is a defining convention in accounts, and investments in other businesses, subsidiaries and in research and development are valued ultra-conservatively. Often, this gives an unrealistic idea of their true value to the business.

Alternative measures

An alternative is to attempt to measure the generation of economic value added. This is defined as the output for any period less the real cost of all the resources consumed in the same period. The main difference between this and the traditional approach is that assets are valued at current values and the cost of capital (including loan capital) is brought into account.

The cost of capital is calculated by considering the opportunity cost of employing that capital elsewhere. It is deducted from the profit before loan interest charges but after tax. The actual interest rate to be used for the cost of capital should be a weighted average of the actual cost of loans and the notional rate to represent a fair return on equity capital.

The economic value added is therefore the value created by the business during the period, after taking into account the return due to the owners to compensate for opportunity costs of other possible investments.

This approach calls for unorthodox thinking – for example, in arriving at a current value for research and development or treating leased assets as part of the total assets of the business. If the asset is used in the business, it should be brought in at its current value.

This still only produces the economic value added for a past period. Future profits and cash flow are of course unknown. However, realistic future cash flow and profit forecasts can be converted to present values by discounting. The present value of future cash flows can be considered as the value of a business over and above its current asset values.

Cash – the ultimate measure

A company may have a high shareholder value, but ultimately the shareholder will only be able to measure that value by cash in his hand. In other words, the only way in which shareholder value can be realised is in cash. This can be by way of dividends paid during his ownership of the shares, plus increase in the value of the shares while he holds them. For quoted companies, this poses no problem, but for unquoted companies, there must be a buyer willing to pay the price for a realistic value of the shares.

FOUR KEY MEASURES OF SUCCESS

In any assessment of the success of a business, certain elements are basic. Below are four key financial indicators which a successful business would be expected to display.

Liquidity

As a business makes profits, the value of the assets of that business increases. The key to success is to ensure that the increase in assets does not occur only in long-term assets such as land and property, machinery and so on. Sufficient assets must be in liquid form to pay short-term liabilities as they become due.

We saw in Chapter 2 the importance of the quick ratio. Chapter 5 dealt with the controls needed to keep liquidity healthy.

Profitability

The key to business survival and success is to make profits. Without this, the business cannot survive.

The simplest measure of profitability is the bottom line of the profit and loss account. However, this measure is rather crude, and does not give insights into the business. To enable action to be taken, further information is needed.

In Chapter 2, we saw how various ratios and percentage analysis techniques reveal how the business is performing and what could be improved. That chapter also showed the calculation of the 'return on capital employed', and the 'return on investment'. These indicate whether your business has performed better than simply putting your money into a bank or building society account.

Finally, the profit and loss account should be looked at in conjunction with the previous year's figures and budgeted figures. The trend of the figures over past years gives useful indicators.

Borrowings

Borrowing is usually needed for businesses to start up or expand. Chapter 10 deals with different types of borrowing in more detail. Borrowing should be appropriate and matched to the purpose for which it is needed.

The long-term borrowing ratio to capital employed reveals the gearing. The significance of gearing is considered in Chapter 10. If gearing becomes too high, some equity capital may be needed to dilute the gearing ratio.

The cost of borrowing is shown as an interest charge in the profit and loss account, and a key concept is interest cover, also considered in Chapter 2.

Cashflow

The old business adage says: cash is king.

However, it is possible to make a profit yet still run into cashflow problems. Cashflow must be actively managed, and Chapter 5 dealt with this in some detail. In a successful business the cashflow is actively managed and is not revealing any shortcomings.

ORGANIC GROWTH

Applying investment principles, an investor would look for organic growth in the value of the business. This means that the business does not rely primarily on acquisitions of other companies to grow but that it produces real growth of its own – in terms of turnover and profit.

The key indicator an investor would look for is the earnings per share and the past record of these.

OTHER CORPORATE VALUES

Many corporate values used as measures of success are not just financial in nature or are easily capable of measurement.

> Corporate values are the guiding principles of the organisation and should not be sacrificed to short-term gain.

These values are largely in the custody of the top levels of management, who are responsible for seeing that they are maintained and communicated to all employees. The ultimate goal is to achieve a state in which the corporate values become shared values – shared between the organisation and the individuals who work there.

A business sharing its values with its employees usually achieves much more, and benefits are seen in greater productivity and better staff relations. Recruitment is easier and staff retention is not so problematic. Staff feel greater job satisfaction and security. Relationships between staff in different departments and in different locations are improved. Managing change or crisis is also smoothed by shared values.

MEASUREMENT OF FUTURE SUCCESS

So far we have looked at historic measures of success. It is, of course, impossible to measure the success or failure of future events. However, a key area of financial management is the appraisal of possible projects or capital investment.

Project and investment appraisal

Certain techniques can be applied to evaluate future projects and make investment decisions.

You need to make informed decisions when faced
with investing significant amounts of money.

These techniques enable you to weigh up possible future benefits (which have an element of uncertainty) against immediate costs (which are far more certain). Below are some situations for which the techniques of project appraisal are appropriate:

◆ Is it better to purchase a new piece of equipment or vehicle rather than continue to use existing older items?

◆ Should I take over or merge with another company? Would the benefits outweigh the cost of acquisition?

◆ Should I produce certain components myself, or continue to buy them in from external suppliers?

◆ Should I pursue the research, development and marketing of a new product or service?

◆ I am faced with two or more alternative projects with roughly equivalent costs, only one of which can be undertaken. Which one should go ahead? (In this case, the decision may involve not only the financial outcome but other critical resource limitations.)

The financial techniques use objective facts and figures. Unknown risk factors inherent in any future project can be the subject of statistical techniques. However, when all these objective facts and figures are presented for a decision, managers still apply their own subjective views of the industry and the economic environment in making a decision. To that extent it will involve 'gut feelings'.

Below are some techniques of project appraisal which may be used individually or in combination.

Payback

This is the simplest measure of appraising a project in financial terms. It may lack some of the sophistication of other methods but it is easily understood. Many businesses – even of substantial size – use this method to appraise projects.

Payback is the measure of the length of time taken to recover the initial investment of money.

Example 7.1

Should you buy a new van, or continue to use the old van? The cost of the new van is £10,000. The additional costs of keeping the old van running over and above the costs of the new van are £200 per month. What is the payback period?

The payback time for this project is 50 months (£10,000/ £200), assuming that the additional costs of retaining the old van remain constant.

Example 7.2

A marketing and advertising campaign costs £50,000. Will the extra sales generated justify the cost? The marketing director believes that the campaign will achieve extra sales of 5,000 units per month with a profit per unit of 50p per unit.

The payback time for this project is 20 months. Note, however, that this calculation assumes that the profit per unit will stay constant. It also introduces constraints of resources – can the business produce 5,000 extra units per month on existing capacity of employees, factory space, machinery, etc.?

The measurement of payback period is relatively easily calculated and easily understood, although certain assumptions have to be made. If cashflow is a major concern, payback time is an important factor. If this is not such a critical factor, you may be able to look further ahead and judge the project on other measures.

However, even this relatively simple measure depends on being able accurately to forecast future outcomes. In the above examples, how certain are the additional costs of running the old van? How achievable are the marketing director's predictions of extra sales?

Despite the drawbacks, it is easily seen that the shorter the payback time, the better chance the project has of success. The size of the project affects the sophistication of the calculations. Certain day-to day decisions involving relatively small amounts of money can probably be calculated on the back of an envelope. More complex ones need a spreadsheet.

Average return

This is another fairly simple to calculate and easily understood method. It calculates the total return over a limited period as a rate of return on the cost of the project spread over that period. Because of its limitations it is only suitable for projects spanning a relatively short period.

Example 7.3

Cost of project £50,000. Length of appraisal period five years. The forecast income from the project is as follows:

	Year 1	Year 2	Year 3	Year 4	Year 5
Gross income	60,000	52,500	50,000	42,500	30,000
Expenses	40,000	35,000	35,000	30,000	20,000
Cash flow	20,000	17,500	15,000	12,500	10,000
Cost of project	10,000	10,000	10,000	10,000	10,000
Net cash flow	10,000	7,500	5,000	2,500	Nil

The total profit from the project is £25,000. Over five years, this averages £5,000 per year. The cost of the project is averaged at £10,000 per year, and the average return is therefore 50%.

However, the drawback of this method is seen if the pattern of the income in the above example were different.

Example 7.4

Cost of project £50,000. Length of appraisal period five years. The forecast income from the project is as below. What is the crucial difference?

	Year 1	Year 2	Year 3	Year 4	Year 5
Gross income	30,000	42,500	50,000	52,500	60,000
Expenses	20,000	30,000	35,000	35,000	40,000
Cash flow	10,000	12,500	15,000	17,500	20,00
Cost of project	10,000	10,000	10,000	10,000	10,000
Net cash flow	Nil	2,500	5,000	7,500	10,000

▶

Here, the total figures are the same, and this method yields the same average result – 50%. However, the difference is that the income starts to build up over the years and most of it is received in the later years.

The real return diminishes because the income is received later. Therefore some more sophisticated method is required to measure the effect of the lapse of time.

Internal rate of return (IRR) and discounted cash flow (DCF)

These methods calculate the effective rate of return generated for the business on the original investment made in a project. The net present value (NPV) of a project can be calculated by these techniques.

They are based on the measurement of future cash values against present cash values. They recognise that money in the hand now is worth more than money in the future.

Compound interest
The measurement of the value of future money as against present money is made using compound interest. The calculation of compound interest is central to working out the IRR on a project.

Example 7.5

If you invest £100 in an account paying 10% interest, at the end of 1 year, it will be worth £110. If you left it undisturbed, after another year, it would be worth £121. This illustrates the compounding effect of interest. The interest is not simply doubled, but there is extra interest on the existing interest. The effect of this gradually increases year by year.

The effect of compound interest can be calculated by means of a formulae as follows:

$$Vn = Vp \times (1+i)^n$$

where:
Vp is the amount of present money, i.e. now;
Vn is the amount of money at the end of year n;
i is the interest rate used;
n is the number of years.

Discounted cash flow
This calculates the net present value (or NPV) of the project to the business now, after discounting future cash flows, using compound interest. The measurement of the difference between present money and future money is called a discount rate and it is the 'mirror image' of the compound interest rate discussed above.

Example 7.6

What is the present value of £121 in two years' time, assuming a discount rate of 10%?

The present value is £100 – the figures are the same as used in Example 7.5.

If the calculation is the mirror image of the compound interest calculation, then we can work out a formula for it.

Using the same definitions as above, the formula for calculating NPV is:

$$Vp = \frac{Vn}{(1+i)^n}$$

This formula can be used to find out the present value of any given amount at any number of years into the future at any given rate of discount. Alternatively, tables exist to give present values, and the present values of future amounts can be read from these tables. Figure 7.1 gives an abbreviated form of such a present value table, giving values up to 14% and up to 25 years, in increments of 1.

Example 7.7

You propose to invest £1 million now to increase production capacity. The additional sales forecast is 100,000 items per year at a selling price of £10 each. The gross profit rate is 40% and the additional overheads are £50,000 per year. There are additional marketing and promotion costs in years 1 and 2 of £50,000 each year.

The cash flow (not discounted) is as follows:

	Cash outflow	Cash inflow
Now	£1,000,000	
Year 1		£300,000
Year 2		£300,000
Year 3		£350,000
Year 4		£350,000
Year 5		£350,000

Now, the discount factors are added at 10%:

	Cash outflow	Cash inflow	Factor	NPV	
Now	£1,000,000		1	£1,000,000	
Year 1		£300,000	0.9091		£272,730
Year 2		£300,000	0.8264		£247,920
Year 3		£350,000	0.7513		£262,955
Year 4		£350,000	0.6830		£239,050
Year 5		£350,000	0.6209		£217,315
				£1,000,000	£1,239,970

Deducting the final columns shows a net present value to the business of £239,970.

Years	1%	2%	3%	4%	5%	6%	7%	8%	9%	10%	11%	12%	13%	14%
1	0.9901	0.9804	0.9709	0.9615	0.9524	0.9434	0.9346	0.9259	0.9174	0.9091	0.9009	0.8929	0.885	0.8772
2	0.9803	0.9612	0.9426	0.9246	0.9070	0.8900	0.8734	0.8573	0.8417	0.8264	0.8116	0.7972	0.7831	0.7695
3	0.9706	0.9423	0.9151	0.8890	0.8638	0.8396	0.8163	0.7983	0.7722	0.7513	0.7312	0.7118	0.6931	0.6750
4	0.9610	0.9238	0.8885	0.8548	0.8227	0.7921	0.7629	0.7350	0.7084	0.6830	0.6587	0.6355	0.6133	0.5921
5	0.9515	0.9057	0.8626	0.8219	0.7835	0.7473	0.7130	0.6806	0.6499	0.6209	0.5935	0.5674	0.5428	0.5194
6	0.9420	0.8880	0.8375	0.7903	0.7642	0.7050	0.6663	0.6302	0.5963	0.5645	0.5346	0.5066	0.4803	0.4556
7	0.9327	0.8706	0.8131	0.7599	0.7107	0.6651	0.6227	0.5835	0.5470	0.5132	0.4817	0.4523	0.4251	0.3996
8	0.9235	0.8535	0.7894	0.7307	0.6768	0.6274	0.5820	0.5403	0.5019	0.4665	0.4339	0.4039	0.3762	0.3506
9	0.9143	0.8368	0.7664	0.7026	0.6446	0.5919	0.5439	0.5002	0.4604	0.4241	0.3909	0.3606	0.3329	0.3075
10	0.9053	0.8203	0.7441	0.6756	0.6139	0.5584	0.5083	0.4632	0.4224	0.3855	0.3522	0.3220	0.2946	0.2697
11	0.8963	0.8043	0.7224	0.6496	0.5847	0.5268	0.4751	0.4289	0.3875	0.3505	0.3173	0.2875	0.2607	0.2366
12	0.8874	0.7885	0.7014	0.6246	0.5568	0.4970	0.4440	0.3971	0.3555	0.3186	0.2858	0.2567	0.2307	0.2076
13	0.8787	0.7730	0.6810	0.6006	0.5303	0.4888	0.4150	0.3677	0.3262	0.2897	0.2575	0.2292	0.2042	0.1821
14	0.8700	0.7579	0.6611	0.5775	0.5051	0.4423	0.3878	0.3405	0.2992	0.2633	0.2320	0.2046	0.1807	0.1597
15	0.8613	0.7430	0.6419	0.5553	0.4810	0.4173	0.3624	0.3152	0.2745	0.2394	0.2090	0.1827	0.1599	0.1401
16	0.8528	0.7284	0.6232	0.5339	0.4581	0.3936	0.3387	0.2919	0.2519	0.2176	0.1883	0.1631	0.1415	0.1229
17	0.8444	0.7142	0.6050	0.5134	0.4363	0.3714	0.3166	0.2703	0.2311	0.1978	0.1696	0.1456	0.1252	0.1078
18	0.8360	0.7002	0.5874	0.4936	0.4155	0.3503	0.2959	0.2502	0.2120	0.1799	0.1528	0.1300	0.1108	0.0946
19	0.8277	0.6864	0.5703	0.4746	0.3957	0.3305	0.2765	0.2317	0.1945	0.1635	0.1377	0.1161	0.0981	0.0829
20	0.8195	0.6730	0.5537	0.4564	0.3769	0.3118	0.2584	0.2145	0.1784	0.1486	0.1240	0.1037	0.0868	0.0728
21	0.8114	0.6598	0.5375	0.4388	0.3589	0.2942	0.2415	0.1987	0.1637	0.1351	0.1117	0.0926	0.0460	0.0388
22	0.8034	0.6468	0.5219	0.4220	0.3418	0.2775	0.2257	0.1839	0.1502	0.1228	0.1007	0.0826	0.0258	0.0219
23	0.7954	0.6342	0.5067	0.4057	0.3256	0.2618	0.2109	0.1703	0.1378	0.1117	0.0907	0.0738	0.0153	0.0131
24	0.7876	0.6217	0.4919	0.3901	0.3101	0.2470	0.1971	0.1577	0.1264	0.1015	0.0817	0.0659	0.0095	0.0082
25	0.7798	0.6095	0.4476	0.3751	0.2953	0.2330	0.1842	0.1460	0.1160	0.0923	0.0736	0.0588	0.0061	0.0054

Figure 7.1. Present value tables

Internal rate of return (IRR)

The next step from calculating the DCF is to find out what interest rate is required to yield a zero NPV. In practice this could be done by iteration – that is, by constant repetition of calculations using different values as 'trial' figures. But there is another way.

A similar alternative is to use the 'function' choice on a spreadsheet. This allows the calculation of IRR and NPV at the click of a button.

Figure 7.2 shows this calculation, which has been done using the function wizard of the spreadsheet. It shows that the IRR of the project is 18.69%.

Now	−£1,000,000	
Year 1	£300,000	
Year 2	£300,000	
Year 3	£350,000	
Year 4	£350,000	
Year 5	£350,000	
Internal rate of return		18.69%

Figure 7.2. Calculation of internal rate of return
(the figures are the same as Example 7.7)

If the IRR figure for a project exceeds the cost of capital to the organisation, the result is favourable. Put another way, if the discount rate used for the DCF calculation is entered at the organisation's cost of capital, then a positive DCF is favourable, since it indicates an IRR in excess of the cost of capital.

Caveat – inflation and the risk factor

In all these calculations, it has been assumed that the

future figures are known and certain. In fact, nothing in the future can ever be certain. Inflation has historically been a constant, although the rates of inflation have varied.

Business is all about risk, and there is always a risk element.

We have examined risk management in Chapter 6. Here, we concentrate on the commercial risk inherent in any business venture, which has more to do with uncertainty than the specific risks seen in Chapter 6. In addition to those risks, there is the simple element of the time factor. The longer a project extends, the greater are the chances of risk factors affecting the result.

There are various methods of analysing the risk element in project or investment appraisal.

Sensitivity analysis
This technique considers the variables affecting the financial result of a project individually to see how changes to these values would influence the outcome. The variables that might affect the outcome of a project are:

◆ initial outlay;
◆ project life span;
◆ sales income from the project:
  – sales volume;
  – sales price;

◆ costs of the project:
- direct, variable costs;
- overhead costs;
- finance costs.

Sensitivity analysis takes each of these variables and compares what effect on the final outcome would result from a variation in the expected figures. In particular, it seeks to discover the 'worst case' scenario for each of these variables before the outcome of the project is a negative value, using the NPV as the yardstick. It can be thought of as a specialised breakeven analysis.

These calculations are rendered easier on a spreadsheet. If a model of the project is constructed on the spreadsheet, substitute values can be entered for individual variables to ascertain the result.

Example 7.8

Using the same data as Example 7.7, carry out the following sensitivity analysis questions:

(a) *What cost of investment would reduce the NPV to zero?*

(b) *What volume of sales would reduce the NPV to zero?*

(c) *What unit price would reduce the NPV to zero?*

(d) *What gross profit rate would reduce the NPV to zero?*

(e) *What level of normal overheads (i.e. excluding the first two years' marketing and promotion) would reduce the NPV to zero?*

(f) *What additional marketing and promotion expenses in years 1 and 2 would reduce the NPV to zero?*

Answers:

(a) £1,239,970 – this is simply the same value as shown in the credit column of the NPV calculations.

(b) 84,175 units (to the nearest 5 units)

(c) £8.42 (to the nearest penny)

(d) 33.67%

(e) £113,300

(f) £188,270 (to the nearest £10)

The above answers have been calculated using a spreadsheet.

This analysis then enables you to discover which are the most sensitive variables in the project – that is, which ones have the least margin of safety.

Example 7.9

From Example 7.8, rank the variable in order of sensitivity (most sensitive first):

1st equal	Sales volume (15.2%)
	Sales price (15.2%)
	Gross profit (15.2%)
4th	Cost of investment (24%)
5th	Normal overheads (126.6%)
6th	Marketing and promotion (276.5%)

The most sensitive variables are those having the lowest percentage variance between the expected figure and the figure that reduces the NPV to zero. In general terms, these variances do not indicate a high-risk level.

Strengths and weaknesses

Sensitivity analysis directs managerial attention to the aspects of the project most sensitive to change. That indicates which areas need more investigation, or which could be the deciding factor in proceeding or abandoning the project.

However, it does not in itself indicate clear decisions about those variables – even the most sensitive ones. Those decisions must be made only after further investigation and groundwork. The other main weakness is that it can only deal with one variable at a time. In reality, variables do not alter one at a time.

Scenario analysis

This is another form of sensitivity analysis. It takes different variables for the project and assigns values to them according to different scenarios. Typically, these scenarios depict:

1. the optimistic view;
2. the pessimistic view;
3. the most likely view.

These produce a range of outcomes in terms of the NPV of the project. However, it does not assign any probabilities to the scenarios. Obviously, the most likely view is the one expected to prevail, but the optimistic and pessimistic views give the 'top of range' and 'bottom of range' of outcomes.

Simulations

This is another extension of the sensitivity analysis idea. It sets out to assign probability values to the range of values assigned to the different variables. A computer is used for this technique, using random selections of values and assigning these to all the different variables, then carrying out multiple iterations of this process – which could run into thousands.

Probabilities and their measurement

Assigning probabilities to events is one of the most subjective areas of risk analysis. However, a degree of objectivity can be obtained. Past experience lends objectivity. Experience will indicate how certain events are likely to turn out. For example, when investing in new machinery or vehicles, past experience gives an indicator of their useful life, the possible events like breakdowns leading to downtime and the regular servicing needed. The sales department will have some idea of the market potential of the product and the sensitivity of the market to price changes.

Past experience, however, is not an error-free guide. New technologies, for example, may dramatically affect the lifespan of machinery. Customers may react differently to the past. Some subjectivity is implicit in all probability assessments.

The results of the simulations are summarised to give a range of outcomes in the form of NPV, and the distribution of the different outcomes within this range.

Example 7.10

A simulation of 1,000 trials on random figures produces the following distribution of results in the range of NPVs between £500,000 and £1,000,000:

▶

£500,000 – £600,000	5%
£600,001 – £700,000	15%
£700,001 – £800,000	30%
£800,001 – £900,000	40%
£900,001 – £1,000,000	10%

This approach therefore gives an idea of the most likely outcome. However, it cannot be assessed simply on the results of the figures overall. The detailed results of each random trial should give an indication of the complex relationships between the variables. For this reason, in simulations, the variables are broken down into more detail than we have so far considered in relation to sensitivity analysis.

Example 7.11

Using the data in Example 7.7, what further breakdown of the variables could be used?

Suggestions:

♦ The investment of £1,000,000 could be broken down into cost of machinery, vehicles, other assets, installation costs, downtime, disruption to existing production and so on.

♦ The additional sales forecast could be broken down into home sales and export sales, and in each of these categories further analysis could be done on the size of the local market and the expected market share. This has an obvious inter-relationship with the marketing and promotion costs.

- The sales price could be further analsysed to test market elasticity of demand and the effect of price increases (or decreases) during the life of the project.

- The direct costs could be broken down into materials costs, labour costs, factory costs, research and development costs, direct overheads and so on. These will have an effect on the gross profit margin.

- The overheads could be broken down to their constituent elements and particular attention paid to finance costs.

- The additional marketing and promotion costs in years 1 and 2 could be tested for the different possibilities of marketing and promotion activities, advertising campaigns and so on.

When carrying out simulations, it is important that the results are not interpreted in a mechanistic way. The results are only as good as the underlying assumptions and probabilities. In the end, human judgement must apply.

Application of risk analysis techniques

The final result of all risk analysis techniques is an estimation of how risky the project will be. When this is decided, it is recognised by adjusting the discount rate used in IRR and DCF calculations, as discussed above. The discount rate to be used in DCF calculations is therefore made up of two elements:

- the basic rate; and
- the risk premium;

The higher the risk is judged, the higher will be the risk premium.

Risk reduction

We have seen how risk analysis affects the appraisal of future projects. However, remember the key principle we have seen several times:

If you can't measure it, you can't control it.

The value of measuring something simply to create a more accurate projection is limited.

The key to management is control.

Therefore there is greater point in analysing and measuring risk if that information is used to reduce risk.

Diversification

Remember the old adage:

Don't put all your eggs in one basket.

A business will reduce its risk if it invests its resources in several projects. If the reason for diversification is risk reduction, then it follows that the different projects in which a business invests should be complementary. That is to say, the risk elements should cancel one another out, as far as possible.

The technical term for this complementarity is the

'coefficient of correlation'. This can be measured by assigning values between -1 and $+1$ to the correlation. A correlation of $+1$ indicates that two projects have exactly equal responses to the determining variables. A correlation of -1 indicates that two projects have exactly equal but opposite responses to the determining variables. A correlation of 0 indicates that there is no relationship at all between the response of two projects to the same variables. The ideal scenario for risk reduction is therefore to choose two projects as near as possible to -1 correlation.

Example 7.12

A civil engineering company can invest in projects for building roads or building railways. If the risk element is government policy relating to the relative importance of roads or railways, then the risk elements would be opposite for each option, as follows:

	Project A Road building NPV	Project B Railway building NPV
Government decisions:		
Favouring roads	£25 million positive	£15 million negative
Favouring railways	£10 million negative	£20 million positive

It can be seen that if the company invests in both projects, then whatever government policy is in force, there is a net positive NPV of £10 million.

There are other risk factors that produce opposite outcomes – such as seasonal businesses. In different parts of the country or the world, seasons could operate to complement each other. Thus, a skiing business could operate in the northern hemisphere for one part of the year and the southern hemisphere season for the other part. A seasonal business could diversify into non-seasonal products or services. Another example of diversification is diversifying from manufacturing goods only into also supplying services related to those goods.

As you take on an increasing number of projects, the relative risk factor of each individual project is correspondingly less. Thus, from this point of view, it *may* be better to invest in two projects with an initial outlay of £1 million each rather than in one project with an initial outlay of £2 million. However, each case must be looked at individually, with an eye to maximising the NPV of all projects.

A further qualifying consideration is the amount of management required for the successful operation of a wide variety of projects. Many businesses find that limited diversification provides the optimum benefit taking into account the management requirements of their core business.

Caveat

The coefficient of correlation is only a *relative indicator.*

It should not be allowed to dictate the choice of projects on its own. Far more important is the return on projects in absolute terms – that is the projects with the best NPV.

Decision time

Once the techniques have been carried out, you must make a decision – the go/no go decision. The decision will be made partly on non-financial factors, including 'gut feeling', partly also on the perception of the risk element and partly on the financial project appraisal.

Hurdle rates

To get a go-ahead decision, the project appraisal is often subjected to benchmarks or hurdle rates. These are standards that the project appraisal must meet to get the go-ahead. These can be simple or complex, being a combination of different factors.

Example 7.13

The project appraisal may show a payback period of five years and an IRR of 20%. The hurdle rates may be set at a payback period of not more than four years, and an IRR of 18%. This project has met one hurdle rate but failed the other.

Hurdle rates should be under constant review. It is usual to demand a project to meet all applicable hurdle rates, but a project could be considered if it met most of the hurdle rates but failed on one only.

The marginal cost of borrowing is often the most appropriate hurdle rate, that is to say the cost of borrowing the next £1. However, particularly for substantial projects incurring substantial borrowing, further borrowing could upset the gearing, and the bank or other lending institution may not be happy at this. It may be more appropriate to use the weighted average cost of capital, known as **WACC**. This takes into account the gearing and the cost of each type of capital – loans and equity.

Example 7.14

	Proportion	Cost	Result
Loan capital	40%	10%	4%
Equity capital	60%	20%	12%
Total	100%		
WACC			16%

In these circumstances, 16% would be a reasonable hurdle rate.

However, this calculation can be taken a step further. Supposing that the organisation could raise 95% of the project cost by loan and the remaining 5% by equity. The calculation would then be, *for this particular project*, as follows:

Example 7.15

	Proportion	Cost	Result
Loan capital	95%	10%	9.5%
Equity capital	5%	20%	1%
Total	100%		
WACC			10.5%

This would appear to give a lower hurdle rate for this particular project than previously. However, the size of the borrowing has to be taken into account. Suppose that the size of the loan required would change the gearing to 50/50. The calculation would then be:

Example 7.16

	Proportion	Cost	Result
Loan capital	50%	10%	5%
Equity capital	50%	20%	10%
Total	100%		
WACC			15%

The WACC is now 15%, which would be a more realistic hurdle rate.

Project comparison

As stated at the beginning of this section, these techniques may also be required to decide between alternative projects. The project appraisals of two or more alternative projects will be looked at side by side to decide which one gets the go-ahead. The normal criteria of payback, DCF and IRR, will be compared.

Comparison of mutually exclusive projects will normally involve comparisons of projects with similar costs, if not similar incomes and periods. However, occasionally, there will be projects of differing magnitudes to compare. The comparisons could be misleading if the IRR is the only factor taken into account. A project with a greater IRR but on a smaller base would provide less money if the figures are looked on as absolutes.

Example 7.17

	Initial cost	IRR	NPV at 15%	Payback
Project A	£500,000	19%	£110,000	4 years
Project B	£100,000	24%	£20,000	3 years

Project B has better ratings on all measurements, but in the end puts less into the business's coffers. As mentioned, it is unusual ▶

to have competing projects with such wide variations of initial cost but this apparent anomaly should be borne in mind.

Another possible treatment of project comparisons of differing magnitudes is to put them side by side and deduct the figures of the smaller one from the larger. This shows what the consequence would be of choosing the larger instead of the smaller. In effect, it appraises the outcome of investing the extra money in the larger project. This can also highlight significant differences compared with 'normal' methods of appraisal. Figure 7.3 shows the comparison of two such projects. The initial comparison would seem to show that project B has a greater IRR and a shorter payback period. However, by calculating the figures on the additional project costs, Project A would be seen as preferable. The NPV is greater, and there is a positive answer to the investment of the additional money in project A.

	Project A	Project B	Difference between Project A and Project B
	£	£	£
Now – cost	– 500,000	– 125,000	– 375,000
Year 1	140,000	75,000	65,000
Year 2	150,000	55,000	95,000
Year 3	175,000	45,000	130,000
Year 4	240,000	25,000	215,000
Year 5	250,000		250,000
Payback	Over 3 years	Under 2 years	Over 3 years
IRR	23%	27%	22%
NVP at 15%	£97,166	£22,337	£74,829

Figure 7.3 Project comparison

8

Phases of Business Life

At each stage in a business's life cycle the finance needs are different and the demands of financial management are also different. Here we look at start-up, growth, merger or takeover, and crisis management.

START-UP

> Every business starts with an idea which has to be developed and tested before any commercial operation can begin.

The usual stages of a start-up and the finance needed are as follows:

♦ *Seed finance.* This is needed to research and assess the commercial viability of the concept, and its development.

♦ *Start-up.* This stage occurs when the product or service is being developed, the business being formed into a company and initial marketing taking place. The product or service has not yet been sold commercially.

♦ *Early stage.* At this stage, the development is completed and further funds are needed for commercial manufacture and selling. Typically, the business is not yet making a profit.

Business angels are wealthy individuals who are willing to make investments into a business based on their own experience and interests. They usually have a particular expertise or interest, and perhaps have retired as senior executives of major companies. Alternatively they may have sold a successful business, and wish to use the proceeds in some other constructive way. They may operate individually or in a small group to provide finance for small businesses.

Because of their background they will often expect to be involved in the business on a 'hands on' basis. Before proceeding therefore, establish their compatibility with the existing management. Put another way, if the business angel is going to be coming in and looking over your shoulder, is he or she the sort of person with whom you can gel?

A business angel will want to see a proposal, and make their own assessment. There are several websites aiming to link businesses requiring capital with business angels. Their addresses can be found in Appendix 3.

GROWTH

> Once a business has started and expands, the most important aspect is the management of working capital.

Overtrading
This is a classic danger for growing businesses, and happens when growth puts a strain on the working capital

requirement. This is because the growth in sales leads to increased stockholding, increased work in progress and increased debtors. These increases are typically not matched by increased credit terms from suppliers, while overhead expenses and direct expenses such as wages need to be paid regularly. This danger has been the downfall of many expanding businesses. The growth stage is typically profitable, but profitability without the cash flow is impotent.

Outside finance is also often needed at the growth stage. Growth often involves the acquisition of new premises, new plant or equipment, new transport. Below is a summary of frequent growth stages and the finance requirements:

◆ *Expansion.* At this stage, a business is trading profitably or breaking even. Further finance may be needed to expand the business or to develop the market, the product or the service further. Additional needs may be:
 – extra working capital;
 – finance for expansion of production facilities;
 – finance for developing the market;
 – finance for introducing more product ranges.

◆ *Mezzanine stage.* This stage is also sometimes known as the bridge stage. Companies undergoing the transition from being privately owned to going public, and possibly becoming quoted on the Stock Exchange, use bridge finance.
 Venture capitalists are often the choice for this stage (see Chapter 11).

ACQUISITIONS AND MERGERS

> Your business may reach the stage where you feel that, in the interests of the shareholders, the business should merge with another or take over another business.

Your company may also be the target of another company's bid to acquire it. Whether in the predator company or the target company, the financial manager's role becomes very important.

Definitions

First, it is useful to define the various terms and jargon used.

♦ *Merger*. This is the combination of two or more businesses of more or less equivalent size. There is generally broad agreement between the management of both businesses about the desirability and the terms of the merger. The outcome is usually the creation of a new company to take over the businesses of the existing ones. All shareholders receive a stake in the new company, pro rata to their existing shares.

♦ *Horizontal merger*. This occurs when a company merges with another company in the same industry and at the same stage of the added value chain. Thus if one retail supermarket chain merges with another, this is a horizontal merger.

♦ *Vertical merger*. This occurs when a company at one stage of the added value chain merges with another at a different stage. Thus if a retail supermarket chain merged with a wholesale grocer, that would be a vertical merger.

- *Conglomerate merger.* This occurs when a company merges with another in a different, unrelated business area. Thus if a retail supermarket chain merged with a motor car manufacturer, this would be a conglomerate merger.

- *Takeover.* This term refers to one company acquiring control of a smaller company. The business of the smaller company is absorbed into the business of the acquiring company. The shareholders in the smaller company may receive a cash payout for their shares or shares in the acquiring company.

- *Predator company.* This describes a company launching a takeover bid for another company.

- *Target company.* This describes the company for which a takeover bid has been made.

- *Bid.* This refers to the terms of offer by the acquiring company.

- *Hostile bid.* This refers to an unwelcome bid. The target company may decide to contest the bid or to accept it. Contested bids often make news headlines.

Why do mergers and takeovers occur?

Company directors may wish to expand their company in the urge to get bigger. Some mergers and takeover bids happen because the managers or directors of the predator company have personal ambitions. If they can manage a larger company, they have greater prestige, power and usually money. These takeover bids are more often contested than others.

However, mergers or takeovers usually happen when there are potential gains. Put another way, the combined businesses of the companies involved should be of greater value than the companies if they continued their separate existences. In what ways might this increased value occur?

1. Economies of scale

A business may be able to make economies of scale in several ways:

Lower administration costs

When a merger or takeover occurs, there are often redundancies. These can happen across the board, but more often most of the redundancies occur in the administration department. Larger companies can often be run by fewer administration staff than two separate companies. This is particularly true as technological advances mean that more work can be automated.

Greater bargaining power

Economies of scale can also be made in the greater bargaining muscle of a larger company. When ordering from a supplier, for example, better terms and cheaper rates can be obtained when the supplier knows that they will have regular large orders from a customer.

2. Elimination of competition

A merger or takeover is often carried out to eliminate competition.

Two or more companies may agree that their competition in the same marketplace is counter-productive. A merger will mean that they can better exploit the market working together. Alternatively, one company may wish to acquire another to gain that company's market share to add to its own.

The larger market share can lead to economies of scale. A larger business may obtain better terms and profit margins than one with a smaller market share.

Caveat
When businesses gain a large proportion of the market share, particularly when this approaches a monopoly, there is less customer choice and the increase in consumer prices often becomes counter-productive. A government body known as the Competition Commission can be invoked to consider whether a particular merger or takeover is in the public interest. If necessary, that body can veto the merger or takeover.

3. Better use of resources
A frequent justification for a takeover is that the management team of the target company has not made the best use of the resources at its disposal and that a new team introduced by the acquiring company can improve on their performance. This type of takeover bid is not

necessarily made by a larger company against a smaller one. This often leads to a takeover battle, where the management of the target company defends its management record, and often improves its performance while the battle is going on.

4. Better use of complementary resources
This rationale often occurs when similar businesses merge, for example:

- one company has better research and development capabilities while the other has better marketing ideas and staff;
- two companies operate in the same business but in different geographical areas.

The combination of the strengths of the two or more businesses provides the impetus for the merger and typically the management of the businesses will be favourably disposed to this type of merger.

5. Use of surplus cash funds

There may be occasions in the life of a company when it has surplus funds without the opportunity to plough those funds back into its own business.

As an alternative to investing the surplus funds in the money market, investing the money in another company may be a viable and profitable use of surplus funds.

6. Diversification

We have seen in Chapter 6 that risk is always present in business. Diversification is a way of reducing risk. A merger or takeover may be seen as a way of diversifying a company's operations and therefore its exposure to risk. Some examples include:

◆ The existing business of a company is seasonal, and a merger or takeover which takes it into another industry which is not so seasonal 'smoothes out' the seasonal variations.

◆ Industries and business sectors go through economic activity cycles, and merger with a company in a different industry could mean that while one business is at a 'low' in its economic cycle, the other is at a 'high'.

The financial management role

In takeover and merger bids and negotiations, the role of the financial manager is crucial.

The three main financial areas are:

◆ valuation of businesses and shares;
◆ vulnerability and resistance to takeover bids;
◆ purchase consideration for a takeover.

1. Valuation of businesses and shares

From the point of view of both the predator company and

the target company, share valuation is important. The main methods used for valuations are those based on:

♦ asset values;
♦ analysis; and
♦ future cash flows.

In all cases there are difficulties of measurement.

Asset values
The following methods are used to value a company's shares.

1. *Balance sheet values.* This is the simplest method. There are three steps, and all the figures can be extracted from the company's latest balance sheet.
   – Take the total gross assets.
   – Deduct the total liabilities to arrive at the net assets of the company.
   – Divide the total net assets of the company by the number of shares, to give the value of each individual share.
   This method is simple and the figure cannot be disputed on the basis of the published balance sheet of the company. However, this method is not the final word because the balance sheet figures for assets and liabilities may have little relation to the market values.

2. *Net realisable values.* This method takes into account the value the various assets would realise if they were sold off piecemeal. It also takes into account the costs (such as auctioneer's fees) of selling off the various

assets. For this reason, this method is sometimes referred to as 'break-up valuation', or 'knock-down valuation'.

This method is not based on the business being a going concern. The values used are what the company might expect on a forced sale of the assets, not the total assets of the business as a whole. The value of the assets therefore would be considerably less than the value on a going concern basis.

3. *Replacement values.* As the name suggests, this method uses the cost of replacing all the assets in their present state. This takes into account current values, and is likely to provide a more realistic estimate of the asset values, particularly in a merger or takeover scenario.

Some items such as machinery, vehicles and so on may be fairly easy to obtain replacement values for. However, other items, particularly intangible assets such as goodwill, patents and brand names can be difficult to value realistically.

Analytical methods
Where a company's shares are not quoted on a recognised market, analytical methods may be used to help put a valuation on that company's shares by comparison with similar quoted companies.

The first task, often the most difficult, is to find suitable comparable companies. First of all, the company must be in the same business sector and industry. It is no good comparing the value of shares in a retail company with those of a bank.

For a fair comparison, the companies should be as similar as possible to each other. For example, its risk profile should be similar. This is to some extent tied in with the management style, although it is difficult to find two companies run in exactly the same way. Similarly, the companies should have a similar growth record and dividend policy.

It is probable that the unquoted company will have a different policy in relation to directors' remuneration from the quoted company. There are many adjustments to make to the bare figures before attempting a comparative valuation.

It is unlikely that the companies to be compared will be of similar size. If a quoted company is being compared with an unquoted company, the quoted company will usually, but not necessarily, have a much larger market capitalisation.

Finally, if all the other factors were matched perfectly, it could not be said that the values of the shares of the two companies are identical. The very fact of the shares being quoted on a recognised market means that those shares are more marketable than non-quoted shares. The degree of marketability is a further factor influencing the value of the shares, and the unquoted company's shares will always be at a discount to the quoted company's shares.

The analytical method involves comparison of two main ratios,
the price/earnings ratio and the dividend yield ratio.

◆ *The price/earnings ratio* is calculated by dividing the
market value per share by the earnings per share, and
we have seen its implications in Chapter 7. A higher
figure means that market sentiment views the company's prospects in a more favourable light. In order to
calculate the value of shares, the equation can be
rearranged so that it is the product of multiplying the
target company's earnings per share by the equivalent
price/earnings ratio.

Example 8.1

Earnings of Unquoted Company Ltd are £2.50 per share. The
price/earnings ratio of Comparable Quoted Company plc is
5.5 times. By multiplying these two figures, we arrive at a
market value of £13.75 per share.

◆ The dividend yield method involves expressing the
gross dividend per share as a percentage of the market
value per share, as seen in Chapter 7. This is obviously
only possible where the market value per share is
known. However, this calculation can be rearranged to
apply the dividend yield of the similar quoted
company to the gross dividend per share to obtain
the market value per share.

Example 8.2

Gross dividend of Unquoted Company Ltd is 50p per share.

▶

> Dividend yield of Comparable Quoted Company plc is 3.5%. By applying this yield to the gross dividend we obtain a market value of £14.28 per share.

Cashflow methods – future dividends
This method of valuing shares is based on the future dividends receivable from those shares. If the value were based only on the dividend to be received in the next year, the value could be expressed in the following equation:

$$\text{Value} = \frac{\text{Next dividend}}{\text{Required rate of return}}$$

However, the value of the shares should not only reflect the next dividend but the entire stream of dividends (in fact, the entire stream of income of any sort) from the shares. As we saw in Chapter 7, net present value and discounted cash flow techniques are based on the theory that future money is not worth as much as present money, and the further into the future, the more the figure is discounted. Applying that to this method of valuing shares, we can arrive at the following formula:

$$\text{Value} = \frac{\text{Div}_1}{(1+R)} + \frac{\text{Div}_2}{(1+R)^2} + \dots \frac{\text{Div}_n}{(1+R)^n}$$

Where:

Div_n = the dividend received in future period n
R = the required rate of return.

However, this model suffers from a couple of drawbacks. First, the future dividends could be projected for an almost infinite number of years. However, the further in the future, the smaller the impact they have on the final result. Secondly, projection of future dividends would assume a constant rate. In reality, company dividends tend to fluctuate. Most companies would hope to be able to show a gradual increase in the rate of dividend, but fluctuations do occur in both directions – up and down.

If we could assume a constant rate of growth of dividends, the value using these methods could be reformulated as follows:

$$\text{value} = \frac{\text{Div}_1}{R - G}$$

where:

G = the constant rate of growth.

Cashflow methods – surplus cash availability
This method is based on future cash available to lenders and shareholders. This is calculated by taking the net cash flow generated by the business (*not* the profit), after deducting payments of tax, dividends and investment in new assets. This remaining cash is available to lenders and shareholders.

The value of the shares in this model is calculated by using the net present value and discounted cash flow techniques, using the cost of capital as the base rate. Once again, problems are encountered in forecasting future events, especially as cash flow is dependent on more than profits. This method arrives at a value of the business as a whole, and this calculated value is then divided by the total number of shares.

As with future dividends, the formula can be expressed to assume a constant rate of growth of cash availability.

The formula for expressing this value is as follows:

$$\text{Value of business} = \frac{\text{Cash availability}}{CC - G}$$

where:

CC = cost of capital;

G = the constant rate of growth of cash availability.

In this method, cash availability is assumed to be for lenders and shareholders. Therefore, the value arrived at is for the business as a whole, but before deduction of the loan creditors and preference shareholders. Those amounts must therefore be deducted to arrive at the amount available to ordinary shareholders.

Many factors in the generation of profit are uncertain, and others are the result of management policy. Other items, including particularly the dividend policy and the amounts invested in new assets or realised from the sale of assets, are even more at the mercy of management policies.

Summary

The different methods of valuing shares produce different figures.

It could be a useful exercise to carry out all the methods to arrive at the range of valuations. Those valuations would then provide the higher and lower extremes. Those extremes would be used in negotiating figures. However, certain methods may be more appropriate than others – everything depends on the individual circumstances, and generalisations are misleading.

2. Vulnerability and resistance to takeover bids

Vulnerability

A takeover or merger affects many people and organisations – not just the target company.

Shareholders, employees, suppliers and customers are all affected positively or negatively by a takeover.

Many businesses therefore pay much attention to their vulnerability to a takeover bid. Surveys have been carried out of the characteristics of businesses which have been acquired. By comparing their business statistics and key ratios with industry averages, certain characteristics have been identified to indicate vulnerability to takeover bids. These include the following:

- lower than average return on capital during the four or five years preceding the takeover;
- lower 'acid test' ratio;
- lower current ratio;
- lower net profit margin before and after tax;
- higher 'growth–resource mismatch' than average.

This last category refers to the fact that if a business has a disparity between resources and growth it will be seen as good value for acquisition. Thus if a company shows

- high growth and low resources or
- low growth and high resources

it will represent good value, even though these two scenarios would seem to be contradictory. In this definition, growth is represented by sales growth, and resources by liquidity and gearing (low gearing representing high resources and vice versa).

In summary, if a business wants to reduce its vulnerability to a takeover, it should maintain good general financial health.

Resistance

> Not all takeover bids are defended or resisted.
> Mergers are less frequently resisted than takeovers.

However, directors may believe it is in their own interests to resist, or that it is in the shareholders' interests. They may also make a defence to influence the predator company to increase its bid.

What methods of defence and resistance can be used? Some defences must by their nature be made before any takeover bid, but others can be made after a bid.

- *Change of status.* A predator company would find it more difficult to acquire shares in a private limited company, which may have restrictions on the sale of shares. Such restrictions could include, for example, a clause stating that shares to be sold must first be offered to existing directors, or existing shareholders. For this reason, the lack of marketability makes their shares of less value than an equivalent public limited company.

- *Establishing employee share option schemes.* Shareholding employees are more likely to resist a takeover bid, since it is more likely that their jobs will be affected. This is more effective when the employees have built up larger shareholdings.

- *Circulating shareholders.* If the management wish to resist a bid, it will often write to all shareholders promptly setting out their reasons for resisting the bid. This sometimes involves disclosing previously confidential information, such as future plans, forecasts, valuations of assets, new contracts and so on. Once disclosed in this way, they are in the public domain.

- *Lessening the company's appeal.* The management may take steps to make the target company less attractive to bidders. Sometimes this could involve taking steps that are in consequence not entirely in the company's highest interest. This is known as 'taking a poison pill', and could involve selling off prime assets. Another term used in takeover jargon is 'the crown jewels', referring to the company's prized assets, sold off as a defensive measure.

Another measure to make the company less attractive is to instigate 'golden parachutes'. These are agreements with directors to pay large amounts to them for loss of office in the event of a takeover. It could also include such tactics as paying large sums to shareholders, thereby reducing the cash balances and increasing the gearing.

♦ *Pac-man defence.* This refers to the target company making a counter-bid for the predator company. This is a difficult strategy when there is a large discrepancy in the size of the predator company and the target company.

♦ *Seeking a different acquirer.* This is known as the 'white knight' defence, where the target company seeks a merger with a company with which it is happier than the predator company. This could happen because of differing management styles or a lack of clear synergy.

Predator action

The predator company may respond to the defences of the target company in other ways. It may circulate the shareholders of the target company with its own explanations or reasoning. It may overcome resistance by increasing its offer. It may even pitch its first bid deliberately low as a negotiating ploy.

The City Code on Takeovers and Mergers

The City Code protects the interests of shareholders of both the predator company and the target company by ensuring that they are given complete information to make a proper decision. In practice this means that shareholders receive an enormous quantity of literature which they do not understand and they have to rely on professional advice to interpret the information.

3. Purchase consideration

When a company wishes to buy another company's shares, it has to devise ways to pay for them.

The most common ways are:

◆ cash
◆ shares in the predator company
◆ loan capital in the predator company

or any combination of these three methods.

Cash

This is the preferred method for the target company shareholders. They receive cash which they then have the choice of reinvesting or not as they wish. They may wish to reinvest in the predator company, or in a different company, or not re-invest at all. They have complete freedom of choice. However, the receipt of cash may trigger a liability to capital gains tax.

A cash offer is also the most easily understood by shareholders. Other offers may require sophisticated knowledge and understanding to make an evaluation.

A cash offer may include part of the consideration in deferred form – cash payments being spread over a period of time. This may lessen the appeal of the bid to the target company shareholders.

From the point of view of the predator company, this method also means that there is no dilution of its capital. However, it does mean that the cash paid for the offer has to be financed. This can be done by:

♦ taking a loan;
♦ making a new share issue (which would involve dilution of the capital); or
♦ selling off assets.

Each of these options may pose difficulties for the predator company.

Shares
This involves issuing to the target company shareholders new shares in the predator company, on some equitable basis to reflect the price to be paid. This may not be as favourable to the target company shareholders as the cash option. They may not wish to retain shares in the predator company. However, the exchange of shares in this way does not trigger a capital gains tax liability.

The number of shares in the predator company given to target company shareholders is determined by the market value of the shares in each of the companies. Thus any fluctuation in the values may seriously affect the offer. In addition, the predator company must ensure that its authorised capital is adequate for the issue of the new shares. If not, special resolutions must be passed and special forms registered at Companies House, adding to the cost of the takeover.

The issue of new shares also means that the capital of the predator company is diluted. There could also be a dilution of the earnings per share if the additional earnings from the acquisition of the new business are lower than the existing earnings per share.

Loan capital
This involves the issue of loan stock or debentures to the target company shareholders. From the point of view of the target company shareholders, this shares some of the disadvantages with the issue of shares. They would not acquire any equity in the predator company, which could be a further disincentive.

However, the loan stock issue could be convertible, so that there is the option to convert into ordinary shares of the predator company at some future date. This could provide relative security in the early years after a takeover, with the chance to participate in the future prosperity of the merged businesses if they are successful.

From the point of view of the predator company, this, like the share issue, is less of a strain on cash resources. However, it does increase the gearing and therefore the financial risk becomes greater.

Management buy-outs and management buy ins
◆ *Management buy-out*. This situation occurs when the existing operating management and/or investors wish

to buy the whole business, a division of the business or perhaps a product line. Specific financing is matched to this, often provided by venture capitalists. In a management buy-out, shareholders must be extra vigilant. The managers involved are of course looking to secure the best deal for themselves, and this could lead them to withhold certain information from the shareholders. Shareholders often seek independent advice in these circumstances.

◆ *Management buy-in.* This is the situation when a group of managers from outside the business wish to buy into the business and run it, or buy into a division of the existing company.

CRISIS MANAGEMENT

There are sometimes occasions when even the best business runs into difficulties.

These difficulties can arise from external sources, such as a natural disaster. In recent history, the foot and mouth crisis affected not only businesses in agriculture and related sectors, but also in tourism. Another external source of difficulties could be the failure of a major customer or supplier, leaving either a bad debt or a lack of vital supplies. Other difficulties can be self-inflicted.

Whatever the reason, there could be significant financial problems, which have to be managed.

The first rule of crisis management is: don't panic!
The second rule is: don't stick your head in the sand. A crisis will not go away – It has to be faced.

Very often external help is needed from the bank or other finance source. The management must not attempt to minimise the crisis, but set out all the facts and suggest a way forward. The bank will be much more likely to respond positively to this open, honest approach.

Short-term measures

A crisis is usually short-term, and short-term measures are required. Once the situation has been retrieved, the short-term measures can be discarded. Below are some of the most common short-term measures that can be adopted.

- *Downsizing.* This involves reducing the scale of operations in one form or another. The most commonly recognised form of this is to reduce the number of employees. However, there are often ways to manage without getting rid of employees. Some solutions are:
  - persuading employees to accept revised working and pay conditions – this can be successful if it is seen to be a temporary measure;
  - outsourcing– some of the tasks done by employees could be done by external sources such as subcontractors and so on;
  - seasonal working – this could be a solution in some businesses.

- *Renegotiating long-term contracts.* Some commitments are long term and their continued presence could be detrimental to survival of the crisis. It may be possible to persuade, say, a landlord of rented property to accept a renegotiated contract for the rent. If the landlord can see that the only alternative to renegotiation may be the failure of the business and the property standing empty, success is likely.

- *Rationalising the supplier base.* Another possibility may be to review the supplier base. Although diversification may be advantageous in many cases, it may sometimes be better in a crisis to concentrate on fewer suppliers and buy in larger quantities. This may give the leverage to negotiate better prices and terms.

- *Cutting budgeted expenditure.* Certain classes of overhead are subject to budget restrictions. Thus it may be possible to reduce expenditure on, say, advertising or research and development as a short-term measure. However, the long-term future of the business must not be endangered by short-term expediencies.

- *Focusing on core activities.* A crisis may lead management to a radical rethink on its activities. It may take the opportunity to redefine its core activities and consider whether any peripheral activities should be curtailed. This can lead to the realisation of surplus assets and/or the redirection of valuable resources, including labour, into the core activities.

  This process can lead to more than a short-term measure, since the business may well find that its financial health improves by concentrating on the core activities.

Releasing locked up capital

In a crisis, many businesses find that they are able to release the capital locked up in long-term assets or underutilised assets.

- *Identifying under-used assets.* Using the techniques described in Chapter 2, it is possible to identify underemployed fixed assets. The sale of those assets could realise some capital, without seriously affecting sales.

- *Sale and leaseback.* This operation involves selling assets to a leasing company, then leasing them back at a fixed rental, payable at regular intervals. It may be possible in this way to realise the capital value of certain assets, without having to dispose of them.

- *Deferring non-essential capital expenditure.* Certain capital expenditure may have been planned and budgeted some time in advance. A careful examination of priorities may result in suspending certain non-essential capital expenditure. Once again, however, the long-term future of the business should not be jeopardised.

- *Selling off surplus assets.* A review of the business prompted by a crisis may reveal certain assets which are surplus to real needs. These could be sold off to raise some capital.

9

Managing Bank Relations

The relationship with your bankers is vital. In this chapter we consider the main areas of that relationship. This involves the personal aspects of how to manage the relationship as well as the technical aspects of presentation of figures. The bank recognises that it is dealing with people, and they will determine how the business operates.

WHAT DOES THE BANK HAVE TO OFFER?

Any business may wish to open a bank account or change its bankers.

> Always think about priorities and what you want from the bank.

For example, a new business starting up may like the idea of free banking for the first year or two. Perhaps working capital requirements may mean that an overdraft renewable on demand is important. It could even be something as simple as the location of the branch, with accessibility to the manager who has authority to take decisions on the account.

Whatever bank is chosen, think long term. You are entering into a long-term relationship which should be stable. Do all the homework beforehand. It is always a good idea to shop around before buying something, and this applies to banking. Before opening an account, see what is available at various banks and how they operate. Special offers may be all very well, but in a long-term relationship, a bank that understands your business and will help it to grow is vital.

Banks are competitive, and it is never a good idea to let banking arrangements simply drift on without any regular review. On the other hand, it is not a good idea to chop and change frequently. However, any bank manager will realise that you are seeking the best possible service from the bank, with the greatest availability of facilities at the most economical cost. For instance, banking coins and notes is usually more expensive in terms of charges than banking cheques. However, this is an area where it may be possible to negotiate lower charges.

Some of the typical business services and facilities offered by banks are:

- free banking for the initial period (up to two years) of a new business;
- guaranteed overdrafts not repayable on demand;
- free business service reviews;
- free business planning and bookkeeping software;
- high interest deposit accounts;
- instant access deposit accounts;
- commercial mortgages;
- credit and debit cards;

- foreign currency accounts and international payments;
- asset finance;
- electronic banking and telephone banking;
- business insurance services;
- free appraisals of business proposals and commercial viability;
- business loans;
- loan guarantee schemes.

HOW THE BANK MANAGER APPROACHES A BUSINESS

When presenting a proposal, it is useful to be able to put yourself in the shoes of the person sitting on the other side of the desk.

How does a bank manager approach a proposition? They will assess the individual and the proposal.

The individual

Character

What is the track record? If the person is an existing customer of the bank, the manager will know whether overdraft limits have been exceeded and so on.

If the person is a new customer, references are taken. The bank manager will possibly ask to see previous bank statements which must cover a consecutive period. If a new customer presents previous bank statements with a gap, there is the immediate suspicion that the gap could be an attempt to hide a problem.

Then the bank manager will form their own opinion about the individual during discussions. Is this individual trustworthy? Do they answer questions openly, or are they guarded? Naturally, this is a personal assessment by the bank manager, but they have much experience in interviewing people and assessing characters.

Capability
The bank manager will also try to gain an idea of the person's capability to manage the business. Again, the bank manager will have much experience of judging people's competence.

When dealing with a new customer, the bank manager will want to investigate further. They may want to visit the business premises, even if working from home. They will form an opinion of the quality of the product and/or service. If there are any key workers, they will want to talk to them. The bank manager will then form an opinion of the state of the business and its recent progress.

The proposal
The bank manager sometimes uses mnemonics to assess the proposal. One that is often used is PARTS. This stands for Purpose, Amount, Repayment, Terms, Security. Below are the sort of questions the bank manager will ask:

Purpose
- What is the money required for?
- Is the purpose reasonable, taking into account all other known facts about the business?
- Is the stated purpose likely to be hiding any other, i.e. is it the *real* reason for requesting the money?

Amount
- Is the amount requested sufficient?
- Does it cover any contingencies and all of the incidental costs connected with the proposal?
- Is the amount requested excessive?
- What is the timing?
- Will the drawdown of the funds be made in instalments?
- Is the proposal realistic in relation to the capital of the business?
- If the proposal is for purchase or construction of an asset, is the bank being asked to fund all of the asset? If not, what proportion is the bank being asked to finance?

Repayment
- How is the customer proposing to make repayments?
- Is the repayment timescale realistic?
- Is any repayment moratorium likely to be necessary?
- Has the customer produced a cash flow forecast taking into account the suggested repayments?
- If the business hits problems, how are the repayments likely to be affected?
- Do the proposed repayments extend beyond the life of the asset?

Terms
- Does the customer understand the bank's terms in relation to interest, charges, commission, arrangement fee and so on?
- Has the customer considered insurance cover for death, accident, health, of the proprietor(s), directors, managers or other key personnel?

Security

- What security is available?
- Does the security carry sufficient value?
- Can the Small Firms Loan Guarantee Scheme help?

Overall

> The bank manager is just as keen as the customer
> for the project to succeed.

If successful, both parties will profit from the deal. However, the bank manager must give the proposal as rigorous an examination as possible. A bad decision can be onerous to both parties. A bank or other lender can probably take a loss without too much pain, but if it goes wrong, it could be catastrophic for the customer. The 'what if?' questions are extremely important.

Maintaining good relationships

The bank realises your business exists to make money just as much as banks do, so the relationship does not have to be one-sided. If the bank does not seem to be forthcoming, take the initiative and take steps to build a better relationship with the bank. Below are a few simple guidelines to maintaining a good working relationship with the bank.

- *Think of the bank as a resource for the business.* The bank is not the enemy to be outwitted or got the better of. The bank can and should be an active partner in helping your business grow. Many have specialist business departments which could help, say, in developing a new idea.

- *Provide the bank with information.* Let the bank have the financial information about your business, which could mean quarterly or half-yearly accounts. Offer to meet them to answer any questions.

- *Keep to agreements made.* Make sure that you can make repayments when they are due. Do not infringe the overdraft limit. The bank can refuse payment of cheques, resulting in a charge on the account, and damage to your reputation.

- *No surprises!* Sometimes going over the bank overdraft limit is unavoidable, or there may be some other bad news. If this is going to happen, tell the bank as soon as possible. Be as precise as possible – tell them how much you are going over the limit and how long it will last. The bank is then unlikely to bounce any cheques.

  The surprises do not have to be bad news. If the bank is not up to date with your business's progress, they may suddenly hear of ambitious expansion plans as a complete surprise. In that case, they will not be as enthusiastic about lending money as if they had been kept up to date regularly and knew that expansion was a possibility.

- *Mollify bad news.* If something has gone wrong, always show what action you are taking to remedy the situation.

- *Demonstrate awareness.* In all dealings with the bank,

show that you are commercially aware, up to date with your business's own transactions, and that your business's finances are actively managed.

- *Never rush the bank for a decision.* They have their own timetable, and will not delay the customer unnecessarily.

- *Think ahead.* The successful end of one negotiation is the end of that chapter, not the end of the story. Look ahead to future development, and start preparing the way for the next negotiations with the bank.

WRITING WINNING BUSINESS PLANS

A lender will want to see a business plan.

This can be a long or short document. The amount of detail will depend on the nature of the project for which finance is required and the amount involved. A lender will not be impressed with a plan that is either too scanty or unnecessarily elaborate.

Personal contact is at least as vital as the written plan.

The plan must convince the lender that you are capable and that the plan is viable. Below are a few practical suggestions:

- Send in the documentation a few days in advance, allowing the bank manager to consider the proposal without undue rush.

- Be prepared to listen to alternative ways of restructuring the proposal.

- A meeting at your premises could be beneficial, but make sure that interruptions are avoided.

- Be prepared for awkward questions. If they come, do not be defensive or aggressive. Answer as openly and honestly as possible. Do not try to bluff.

- Do not accept any comments not understood or disagreed with. Ask questions to clarify points which seem to be unclear.

- Do not agree to too much security. Work out the bank's maximum exposure to loss and agree to that figure. If the bank asks for double that amount, it is too much.

- Try to avoid giving personal guarantees.

- Concentrate on getting the proposal accepted first, then move on to negotiating terms and rates.

- Be prepared to negotiate for favourable terms – do not threaten.

- Make a summary at the end of the meeting of what has been agreed. Follow it up in writing.

People

The lender must be convinced that you are trustworthy and capable of managing the business in general and the particular project for which finance is sought. The business plan must give enough information on the personal level.

Proposal

The lender must be convinced that the proposal is sound and commercially viable. In addition, the lender must see how the proposal fits in with the business as a whole and if the rest of the business could affect its viability. The business plan must, therefore, show that you have done your homework, and that, as far as possible, all the 'what-ifs' have been covered.

Contents of a business plan

Every situation is unique, so there can be no hard and fast way of making a business plan to be adhered to in every case.

However, below are the elements seen in most cases.

1. Summary

1.1 Introduction to the proposal and business plan. State clearly and simply why the money is needed and what it will be used for. Give a thumbnail sketch of the business in its present state – what its activities are, who runs it and a brief summary of figures. Three figures will be sufficient here – latest annual turnover, profits, and net assets.

1.2 If the proposal is for a new business, give a brief summary of what activity the business will carry on and the projected figures for the initial period – turnover, profit and net assets.

Note. This section should be brief, to give the lender a quick overview which they can keep in their mind as an outline map.

2. The proposal

2.1 Give details of what the money is for, detailed costings of all items and what form of finance is proposed.

2.2 Provide a detailed timetable for the acquisition of all items for which funding is sought, and a timetable for the integration of these into the business.

2.3 Provide a timetable for repayment, building in any moratorium you think may be necessary.

3. Management

3.1 Give details of the experience and qualities of the owners, directors or managers of the business.

3.2 If the proposal is for a new business, emphasise why the owner(s), directors or managers are qualified to make the new business succeed, and how they can work together.

3.3 If the proposal is such that new management expertise will be hired, give details of the profile of the person wanted to recruit, or the person in mind for the job.

3.4 Give details of any other specialised help or expertise available – such as business mentors, business angels and so on.

3.5 If the proprietor(s), directors or managers are nearing retirement age, give details of the proposed succession.

4. Product and/or service

4.1 Give full details of the activities of the business. The main business could be manufacturing, selling (retail or wholesale) or service. Increasingly, many businesses have a mixture of activities, which could include any combination of these three.

4.2 If there is a diversity of activities, indicate which is the core activity, and which are by-products or secondary activities. If, as is often the case, one activity depends on another, and neither could properly be carried out in isolation, make this clear. Try to show how the different activities are linked, and what would be the effect on one activity if the other suffered a downturn.

4.3 Indicate as fully as possible the range of products or services concerned, and the possibility for developing new ones.

5. Marketing

5.1 Convince the lender that the business knows the market for its products or services, and that it knows its existing and/or potential customers.

5.2 First, give an idea of the size of the global, national or local market in the product or service. Even if the business does not aspire to take over the whole market, the lender must be convinced that it will be able to make some impression on the market.

5.3 If the market is a growth area, state the reasons for believing this. Convincing the lender that the business is operating in a growth area will boost the chances of a successful proposal.

5.4 Next, state what sector of the market is targeted. For instance, *The Times* and *The Sun* are two different types of newspaper aimed at different sectors of the newspaper reading market. Avoid making value judgements about any sector of the market. *The*

Times reader may be different to the *Sun* reader, but neither is better or worse than the other in terms of market sector.

5.5 Specify in more detail the customer or client profile. For instance, if selling computer hardware or software, the typical customer may be small or medium-sized professional businesses (e.g. accountants, architects, solicitors and so on). The more specialised your product or service, the more specific is likely to be the typical customer profile.

5.6 Specify the competition. Give as much detail as possible on competitors' turnover, number of staff, geographical spread, and growth or decline in recent years.

5.7 Give details of the pricing structure of the products or services.

6. Sales

6.1 Convince the lender that the product or service will sell. Emphasise its USP (unique selling point).

6.2 Give details of advertising campaigns and an idea of the advertising budget.

6.3 Give details of any special present or future promotions. Targeting promotions is particularly useful.

6.4 Give details of the salesforce, and how and where they sell.

6.5 Pricing of the product or service is most important. Give full details of any discounts, special offers or reductions.

7. Operational

7.1 Give details of the location, type of accommodation

and tenure of all business premises. Give details of the length of leases, outline of the terms of leases, and in particular when any rent reviews become due.

7.2 Give details of the main fixed assets of the business – tangible and intangible.

7.3 Give details of staffing levels and experience of existing staff at all levels. If further staff are needed for the project, give details of the expected number required and at what levels.

7.4 Give details of insurance cover – what risks and the amount of cover.

8. Short-term, medium-term and long-term goals

8.1 Short-term – give a detailed forecast of profits and a detailed cash flow projection for a one-year period.

8.2 Medium-term – give a less detailed forecast of growth and profits over the next five years, with a cash flow projection.

8.3 Long-term – give details of your vision of the future development of the business over the next five to ten year period.

9. Financial details

9.1 Give details of the last three years' accounts figures, showing trends.

9.2 Provide a detailed profit forecast and cash flow projection for the coming year.

10. Security

10.1 Provide full details of anything offered as security. If it is a freehold property, provide an up-to-date survey and/or valuation.

CASH FLOW FORECASTING

A cash flow forecast is an essential part of a
business plan and borrowing proposal.

It sets out for a specific period (usually one year for the
short term) the forecast receipts and payments of the
business, and presents these, usually with monthly
balances, in the form of a table.

Case study 9.1

This case study shows the cash flow forecast for one year
of a company running a hotel – The Supa-Dupa Hotel
Ltd. The hotel is in a resort area where much of the trade
is seasonal. In the process of trying to maximise its profit
by increasing the usage of the hotel all year round, it has
identified a potential market for a 'health and fitness
centre', by converting underused rooms in the hotel into
this centre (essentially a gym) to be opened adjacent to the
hotel's swimming pool. The centre and swimming pool
would then be opened to non-residents all year round.
The cash flow forecast and profit projection are to
accompany the business plan and proposal to the bank
for the finance of this project. The cash flow forecast is
shown in Figure 9.1.

Year ended 31 December 20xx						
	Jan	Feb	Mar	Apr	May	Jun
Income:						
Accommodation	13,750	13,750	13,750	16,600	16,600	16,600
Food	4,600	4,600	4,600	5,500	5,500	5,500
Bar sales	2,300	2,300	2,300	2,750	2,750	2,750
Sundry sales	920	920	920	1,100	1,100	1,100
Health club						
Bank loan		15,000		20,000		15,000
TOTAL	21,570	36,570	21,570	45,950	25,950	40,950
Payments:						
Food costs	4,750	2,300	2,300	2,300	2,750	2,750
Drinks costs	2,625	1,150	1,150	1,150	1,375	1,375
Sundry purchases	1,375	690	690	690	825	825
Wages	3,500	3,500	3,500	4,200	4,000	4,200
Directors' salaries	6,500	6,500	6,500	6,700	6,700	6,700
Cleaning	800	800	800	800	800	800
Laundry	500	500	500	500	500	500
Rates and water	1,250			1,350	1,350	1,350
Light and heat		2,500			2,800	
Property repairs	500	200	4,000	200	300	
Equipment mtce.	400	450	450	500	550	500
Insurance						9,000
Transport	550	550	550	550	600	3,600
Advertising			3,000	3,000		
Professional fees			4,500			
Sundry expenses	200	200	200	200	200	200
Bank charges			750			750
Finance charges	400	400	400	400	400	400
Capital expenditure		15,000		20,000		15,000
Loan repayments			225	225	525	525
Dividends			20,000			
Tax paid						
	23,350	34,750	49,515	42,765	23,675	48,475
Net inflow/outflow	−1,780	1,830	−27,945	3,185	2,275	−7,525
Opening balance	−5,000	−6,780	−4,950	−32,895	−29,710	−27,435
Closing balance	−6,780	−4,950	−32,895	−29,710	−27,435	−34,960

Figure 9.1. Cash flow forecast – the Supa-Dupa Hotel Ltd

	Jul	Aug	Sep	Oct	Nov	Dec
			Year ended 31 December 20xx			
Income:						
Accommodation	40,700	50,600	40,700	31,600	23,750	31,600
Food	13,600	13,600	13,600	10,500	7,900	10,500
Bar sales	6,800	6,800	6,800	5,250	3,950	5,250
Sundry sales	2,720	2,720	2,720	2,100	1,580	2,100
Health club	2,000	2,000	2,000	1,500	1,500	1,000
Bank loan						
TOTAL	65,820	75,720	65,820	50,950	38,680	50,450
Payments:						
Food costs	2,750	6,800	6,800	6,800	5,250	3,950
Drinks costs	1,375	3,400	3,200	3,400	2,625	1,975
Sundry purchases	825	2,040	2,040	2,040	1,575	1,185
Wages	6,200	6,900	6,400	5,900	5,500	6,000
Directors' salaries	6,700	6,700	6,700	6,700	6,700	6,700
Cleaning	800	900	900	900	800	800
Laundry	500	500	500	500	500	500
Rates and water	1,650	1,650	1,650	1,650	1,650	1,650
Light and heat		3,200			3,400	
Property repairs						2,500
Equipment mtce.	500	500	500	500	550	500
Insurance						
Transport	600	600	600	600	550	550
Advertising	1,000				2,400	
Professional fees						
Sundry expenses	200	300	200	200	200	200
Bank charges			750			750
Finance charges	400	400	400	400	400	400
Capital expenditure						
Loan repayments	750	750	750	750	750	750
Dividends						
Tax paid			60,000			
	24,250	34,640	91,390	30,340	32,850	28,410
Net inflow/outflow	41,570	41,080	−25,570	20,610	5,830	22,040
Opening balance	−34,960	6,610	47,690	22,120	42,730	48,560
Closing balance	6,610	47,690	22,120	42,730	48,560	70,600

Figure 9.1 Cash flow forecast – the Supa-Dupa Hotel Ltd (cont.)

What are the processes involved in creating a cash flow forecast?

1. First make a realistic projection of the profit and loss account for the year. This involves making assump-

tions about the various elements of the profit and loss
account (e.g. sales volume, gross profit rate, levels of
overheads and rates of cost increase and so on) and
then quantifying them. This is shown in Figure 9.2.

Year ended 31 December 20xx		
	£	£
Income:		
Accommodation	300,000	
Food	100,000	
Bar sales	50,000	
Sundry sales	20,000	
Health and fitness club	8,000	
		478,000
Expenses:		
Food costs	50,000	
Drinks costs	25,000	
Sundry purchases	15,000	
Wages	60,000	
Directors' salaries	80,000	
Cleaning	10,000	
Laundry	6,000	
Rates and water	15,000	
Light and heat	12,000	
Property repairs	8,000	
Equipment mtce.	6,000	
Insurance	8,000	
Transport	10,000	
Advertising	9,000	
Professional fees	5,000	
Sundry expenses	2,500	
Bank charges	3,000	
Loan interest	4,000	
Finance charges	4,800	
Depreciation	20,000	
		353,300
Net profit before tax and dividends		124,700
Tax	60,000	
Dividends	20,000	
		80,000
Retained profit		44,700

Figure 9.2. Profit projection – the Supa-Dupa Hotel Ltd

2. The assumptions are the most critical part of the projected profit and loss account and the cash flow forecast. They must be explained in as much detail as possible. This is shown in Figure 9.3.

Year ended 31 December 20xx

Capital		£	
Loan from bank		50,000	
Draw down – February		15,000	
April		20,000	
June		15,000	

Repayments over ten years at 8%

March–April repayments	capital	125	(15,000 over 10 years)
	interest	100	(8% p.a. on 15,000)
		225	
May–June repayments	capital	292	(35,000 over 10 years)
	interest	233	(8% p.a. on 35,000)
		525	
July–Dec repayments	capital	417	(50,000 over 10 years)
	interest	333	(8% p.a. on 50,000)
		750	

Capital expenditure

Conversion work for health and fitness centre:

		£
Progress payments	February	15,000
	April	20,000
Equipment		15,000

Income

Accommodation	Number of rooms	Charge per night £	Occupancy rate %	Number of nights	Projected income £
Low season					
Superior double rooms	9	50.00	36	120	19,440
Standard double rooms	17	40.00	42	120	34,272
Single rooms	2	30.00	20	120	1,440
Mid season					
Superior double rooms	9	60.00	44	153	36,353
Standard double rooms	17	50.00	52	153	67,626
Single rooms	2	35.00	35	153	3,749
High season					
Superior double rooms	9	72.00	84	92	50,077
Standard double rooms	17	62.00	85	92	82,423
Single rooms	2	45.00	58	92	4,802
TOTAL					300,182

Food
Food income is approx. 1/3 accommodation income based on previous year.
Bar sales
Bar sales are approx. 50% food income based on previous year.
Sundry sales (postcards, books, confectionery etc.)
Sundry sales are approx. 40% of bar sales based on previous year.
Health and fitness centre
Income should start in July, after completion of the work. Based on initial offer of annual subscription of £80 per person, or £120 per couple, with single visits at £5 per session.
Expenditure
All regular bills are paid monthly, with one month's credit taken.
Food costs
Food costs are 50% of food income.
Drinks costs
Drinks costs are 50% of bar income.
Sundry purchases
Sundry purchases are 75% of sundry sales.
Wages and salaries
General hotel staff consists of a core number of workers, with additional seasonal workers. One extra person will be taken on when the fitness centre opens.
Cleaning and laundry
These expenses are evenly spread through the year, with a slight increase in laundry during the high season.
Business rates and water
The business rates are due to increase once the fitness centre is built.
Property repairs
The majority of the repairs are done in the least busy times – February and November.
Equipment maintenance
Equipment maintenance is paid monthly on various contracts, plus occasional small repairs.
Insurance
Insurance is paid annually in June. The cover and premium will increase when the fitness centre is built.
Transport
The business owns three vehicles. The tax and insurance are paid in June.
Advertising
The main advertising is done through the tourist board and is paid in October each year for the following season. Then, further newspaper advertising is carried out in February and March. There will be additional local advertising for the opening of the new fitness centre.
Professional fees
This consists mainly of the accountancy fees.
Bank charges
These are charged quarterly.
Finance charges
These are payments on an existing hire purchase contract.
Dividends
These will be payable in March.
Tax
This is payable in September on the profits of the previous year.

Figure 9.3. Basis for figures for profit projection
and cash flow forecast

3. Next, make adjustments to the annual figures to arrive at the actual amounts expended during the year. This means making the accrual adjustments at the beginning and the end of the year. Non-cash items like depreciation must also be adjusted. This is shown in Figure 9.4.

	£						
Accommodation income	300,000						
Adjust – deposits received in advance							
at beginning of year	−30,000						
at end of year	40,000						
	310,000						
Health and fitness centre	8,000						
Adjust – income in advance	2,000						
	10,000						

	Per Fig.9.2	Adjust opening creditor	Adjust closing creditor	Adjust opening prepay	Adjust closing prepay	Adjust non-cash item	Total
	£	£	£	£	£	£	£
Expenses							
Food costs	50,000	3,000	−3,500				49,500
Drinks costs	25,000	1,500	−1,700				24,800
Sundry purchases	15,000	1,000	−1,200				14,800
Wages	60,000	1,000	−1,200				59,800
Directors' salary	80,000	800	−1,000				79,800
Cleaning	10,000	500	−600				9,900
Laundry	6,000	400	−400				6,000
Rates and water	15,000			−1,200	1,400		15,200
Light and heat	12,000	1,100	−1,200				11,900
Property repairs	8,000	500	−800				7,700
Equipment mtce.	6,000	400	−500				5,900
Insurance	8,000			−8,000	4,000		9,000
Transport	10,000			−1,000	900		9,900
Advertising	9,000			−1,000	1,400		9,400
Professional fees	5,000	4,500	−5,000				4,500
Sundry expenses	2,500						2,500
Bank charges	3,000						3,000
Loan interest	4,000					−4,000	0
Finance charges	4,800						4,800
Depreciation	20,000					−20,000	0
Tax	60,000						60,000
Dividends	20,000						20,000
Totals	433,300	14,700	−17,100	−6,200	7,700	−24,000	408,400

Figure 9.4. Adjustments to profit and loss figures from Figure 9.2

4. Next, incorporate capital items in the cash flow forecast. This includes expenditure on fixed assets, repayments of loans or hire purchase contracts, payments of tax and dividends. Incoming cash should also be shown, including loans received. The amounts of income and expenditure are allocated to the months in which they should become due for payment.

5. The inflowing and outflowing cash is then totalled for each month, and adjusted on the opening bank balance. The projected bank balance is then shown at the end of each month and carried forward to the next month, and the maximum overdraft facility needed is shown. In this example, it occurs in March, when the overdraft is projected to reach nearly £33,000. However, by the end of the year, the balance in credit at the bank has recovered to stand at over £70,000. This will be needed to pay the dividends and the tax in the next year. This pattern is common in seasonal businesses, and points to the need for treasury management, by investing surplus cash until it is needed.

⑩

Loan Capital, Overdrafts and Working Capital Financing

Small businesses sometimes need loan capital or short-term finance. Here we introduce the concept of capital structure and the effect of the gearing ratio. We examine ways of raising long-term and short-term finance and also look at leasing.

GEARING AND CAPITAL STRUCTURE

Capital structure refers to the relationship between equity capital and loan capital.

> Gearing is a key indicator of a company's financial structure and refers to the relative proportions of equity capital and loan capital.

If the proportion of loan capital to equity capital is high, the company is said to be high geared. Generally, the dividing line between high and low geared companies can be taken as 50%.

Example 10.1

		£
XYZ plc –	Equity capital	5,000,000
	Loan capital	15,000,000
	Total capital	20,000,000

The gearing is the loan capital (£15,000,000) expressed as a percentage of the total capital (£20,000,000). This is 75% – therefore high geared. If the figures were reversed and the loan capital were £5,000,000, the gearing would be 25%.

The significance of high gearing is that if profits increase, the amount of loan interest paid remains the same and the profit available to the equity shareholders increases. This effect is much more marked in a high-geared company than in a low-geared company.

Example 10.2

High-geared company	£
Profits before interest charges	5,000,000
Interest charges on loan capital of £15,000,000	
at 10%	1,500,000
Balance of profit for equity shareholders	
(nominal £5,000,000)	3,500,000

The return to equity shareholders is 70% on the nominal share capital.

Low-geared company	£
Profits before interest charges	5,000,000
Interest charges on loan capital of £5,000,000	
at 10%	500,000
Balance of profit for equity shareholders	
(nominal £15,000,000)	4,500,000

This time, the return to equity shareholders is 30% on the nominal share capital.

Thus, with high gearing, the risks and rewards are potentially greater for the equity shareholders. This is significant when the profits are lower.

Example 10.3

High-geared company	£
Profits before interest charges	1,000,000
Interest charges on loan capital of £15,000 at 10%	1,500,000
Loss	500,000

Low-geared company	£
Profits before interest charges	1,000,000
Interest charges on loan capital of £5,000,000 at 10%	500,000
Balance of profit for shareholders (nominal £15,000,000)	500,000

This time the contrast is between a loss, which means no returns for the equity shareholders, and a profit. Although the profit return on equity capital is only 3.3%, it is at least a profit.

A company's capital structure is therefore the division between the shareholders, who are the members of the company, and the lenders, who are creditors of the company. Interest paid on loan capital is deductible from the company's profits for tax purposes, whereas dividends have to be paid out of profits.

TERM MATCHING

A sound financial principle is that of matching the term of any form of loan or borrowing as far as possible to the expected life of the asset or project which it finances.

Example 10.4

♦ The purchase of freehold property is financed by a mortgage secured on that property.

♦ Renting premises also remains a viable option in certain circumstances, particularly where a project may require premises of some sort – say, for retail sales – but the project life is uncertain.

- ◆ Financing general working capital is best done by bank overdraft facilities.
- ◆ Factoring or invoice discounting is a suitable method of financing book debts.
- ◆ Purchase of fixed assets other than freehold property can be done by loans from banks or other sources.
- ◆ Hire purchase or finance leases are other ways of financing fixed assets such as equipment or vehicles.

RAISING LONG-TERM LOAN CAPITAL

Loan capital is provided by lenders who loan money to the company on terms set out in their contract with the company. Therefore:

- ◆ providers of loan capital (lenders) are not members of the company;

- ◆ lenders have no further claim on the assets of the company other than as provided by the terms of their contract with the company;

- ◆ lenders have a prior claim on the company, and their demands must be met before any proceeds can be paid to shareholders.

- ◆ interest paid on loan capital is tax deductible.

Risk

Lenders have a prior claim on the assets of the company, and to that extent, their risk is lower than shareholders' risk.

However, there is always a certain degree of risk inherent in investing money in a company, in whatever form.

Independent credit-rating agencies, such as Moody's or Standard & Poors, make assessments of the risk categories of loan capital of companies. Their categorisations follow similar lines to each other – from AAA (Standard & Poors) or Aaa (Moody's) to C (both companies). The triple A rating indicates the lowest risk, and the C rating indicates the greatest risk. In this context, the risk being assessed is the risk of interest payments not being made and the repayment of the capital being defaulted on. The common name given to the lower risk grades is 'junk bonds'.

To compensate for the risk, the interest rate offered on lower grade loans is generally higher than that offered on the least risky loans.

Security
If there is a risk element, it is natural that investors should seek some form of security for the money they have invested. This is frequently achieved by a charge over the assets of the company, which means a legal right to use those assets to satisfy their debt.

Charges
There are two types of charge:

◆ *Fixed charge* – the lenders have a charge over specific assets of the company;

- *Floating charge* – the lenders' charge over the assets is not related to any specific assets but 'floats' over the assets generally. If the company defaults on payment, the charge 'crystallises'. When this happens, the lenders have the right to seize assets and sell them to repay their loans.

> Assets over which a charge is held should be easily realisable, non-perishable and have a high value in relation to their size.

The most readily realisable and suitable asset is land or property. Its value is easy to measure and does not tend to decline in normal circumstances.

Loan covenants

A further form of security is provided by covenants (that is, conditions) written into the loan contract. These impose certain obligations on the company, giving additional security to the lenders. Below are some typical conditions:

- The company must send the lenders financial reports.

- The company must not issue any additional loan capital without the permission of the existing lenders.

- If any assets are subject to a charge, those assets must be specifically insured.

- The company must not dispose of certain assets without the permission of the lenders.

◆ Certain payments, such as dividends to ordinary shareholders or payments to directors, should be subject to restrictions.

◆ There should be minimum and maximum levels for certain key ratios such as liquidity or gearing.

Personal guarantees

In some circumstances, lenders may seek personal guarantees from directors or owners of the company, or from some third party. This type of security is most applicable to private companies (see the distinction between private and public companies in Chapter 11).

Types of loan capital

A company may raise its loan capital in different forms.

Subordinated loans

◆ A company may issue different classes of loans.

◆ The rights of some classes, while still ranking above shareholders, may be subordinated to a higher class of loans.

◆ Subordinated loans are thus seen to be of a slightly higher risk than the 'senior' loans and would therefore be expected to carry a higher rate of interest.

Debentures

◆ Debentures are a form of loan established by a trust deed.

◆ Debentures normally carry a fixed and/or floating charge over some or all assets of the company.

- For publicly quoted companies, debentures are often quoted on the Stock Market.

Redeemable or irredeemable loans

- Redeemable loans have a fixed date on which they are repayable. The repayment is usually at par (that is, the nominal amount at which they were issued).

- Irredeemable loans have no fixed date for repayment.

Bearer bonds

- If a loan is issued on a bearer bond, the holder is not registered with the company. However, the holder of the bond is regarded as the owner, and coupons attached to the bonds give the right to receive the interest, which is often paid annually.

Deep discount bonds

- This is a form of redeemable loan capital which allows the company to offer a lower rate of interest than usual.

- It compensates for this by offering the bonds at a discount to the nominal value at which they are to be repaid.

> ### Example 10.5
>
> A company issues a deep discount bond with a fixed life of 15 years at an initial price of 85% of the redemption value. That is, the bond is offered at £85 for every £100 nominal value. In simple terms, this means that there is one per cent of added capital value for every year of the life of the bonds, and the interest rate can be one per cent lower to compensate for this.

Investors may often be attracted to this form of bond because of its tax treatment.

Convertible loans

A convertible loan gives the lender the option to convert the loan to equity shares at a fixed price at specified future dates.

The lenders remain creditors of the company until conversion takes place. If the lenders convert the loan into shares, they become members of the company with the same rights and risks as other shareholders of the same class of shares. Conversion to shares is not compulsory, so the lender only takes advantage of the conversion rights if the share price at the conversion date is favourable.

From the investor's point of view, this offers a good opportunity to participate in any future increase in the value of the shares of the company.

From the company's point of view, it can:

- economise on the costs of redemption;
- use this method to reduce its gearing; and
- offer lower rates of interest on convertible loans.

As against these benefits, the conversion of a large amount of loan could dilute the control and possibly the future earnings of shareholders.

Warrants

♦ Warrants are instruments by which the holder has the right (not the obligation) to buy shares in the company at a fixed price at specified future dates.

♦ The warrants do not give the right to any other benefit from the company and no interest is paid on them.

♦ This method is one way in which the company can raise capital with no immediate cost (in the form of interest payments). The cost comes later.

♦ Warrants are sometimes issued in conjunction with loan capital and sometimes to existing shareholders on the basis of their present holding.

Mortgages

♦ A mortgage is a loan secured on the security of freehold property.

♦ Normally, mortgages are provided by large financial institutions with strict conditions.

♦ Mortgages are long-term lending for the purpose of acquiring or improving the property on which the loan is secured.

RAISING SHORT-TERM FINANCE

Overdrafts

The general rule of term matching means that an overdraft facility should not be used for long-term finance or financing a specific asset. Use an overdraft for financing working capital – its traditional use. Bank managers will usually not agree to an overdraft for other purposes.

The cost of an overdraft is usually more than for a loan in terms of its interest rate and the annual review and arrangement fee. However, because of the nature of an overdraft, its overall cost can be less than a loan. The amount of an overdraft varies from day to day as the account is used for paying bills and receiving money paid in. Thus you may have an overdraft facility for, say, £50,000. However, during the course of your business, the balance may be anywhere up to that limit (and occasionally beyond it). The account may even go into credit, rather than being overdrawn.

Overdraft interest is calculated on whatever the balance is on a daily basis, not the amount of the facility. Thus interest is only charged on the amount of the facility actually used. A loan is for a fixed term with fixed repayments, and the interest is charged on the whole amount outstanding, according to the agreement.

Factoring and invoice discounting

Factoring and invoice discounting are forms of finance based on the value of book debts.

They work in essentially the same way. The business assigns its book debts to the finance company. The finance company provides a proportion (typically 80%) of the value of all invoices by payment as soon as the invoices are raised and sent to customers. When the customers pay the invoices, the business receives the balance of the value of the invoices, less the finance company's charges.

The essential difference between factoring and invoice discounting is that the factoring company takes over the administration of the sales ledger for the business. Invoice discounters do not do this. Thus the charges for factoring are more than for invoice discounting. For the same reason, invoice discounters will generally only take on businesses with a larger turnover, unless they have confidence in the quality of sales ledger administration. Smaller businesses therefore are more likely to find factors to provide finance in this way. Certain businesses, such as builders, are excluded from this form of finance.

Different types
This finance is provided in two types:

◆ recourse arrangements, in which bad debts are recovered against money advanced to the business;

◆ non-recourse arrangements, in which the finance company agrees to absorb any bad debts. Naturally, this type of arrangement is more expensive than recourse.

Invoice discounting comes in two types:

◆ *Confidential invoice discounting.* Because the invoice discounter does not take over the administration of the sales ledger, there is no need for the business's customers to know of their existence.

◆ *Disclosed invoice discounting.* In this case, an 'assignment notice' is printed on the invoices. This is a statement that the debts of the business have been assigned to the invoice discounter to whom payment is made. If the invoice discounters do not have as much confidence in the business's administration, they may insist on disclosed invoice discounting.

Suitability

Factoring or invoice discounting is particularly suitable for rapidly expanding businesses.

As a business expands, the working capital requirement expands as the gap between current assets and current liabilities becomes greater. In fact, this period of expansion can lead to overtrading. Cash becomes squeezed and the business cannot pay its debts on time. Many businesses have failed because of this.

Either insufficient control over the elements of working capital or lack of planning for this vital growth stage causes this. The lack of control can arise through administrative systems or staff not being able to cope adequately with the greater volume of transactions generated during a period of rapid growth. The lack of planning can happen when management fails to foresee the growth or does not plan specifically for it. The growth then takes them by surprise. They overcommit the resources of the business and find themselves unable to cope.

This type of finance is also sometimes seen in management buy-outs to provide an additional tranche of finance to reduce the reliance on other funding. It can be part of a more flexible financing structure.

Operational details

Factors and invoice discounters will vet client businesses before taking them on, and then check procedures and administration regularly. They will also be looking for such things as the way in which the business relates to its customers, including the level of customer complaints, and the frequency of issue of credit notes. Invoice discounters will carry out a review, akin to a full audit, of the business. They are also more likely not to take on a client business until it has an established track record and shows a sound financial position on its balance sheet.

> Choosing a finance company to carry out this service need not be onerous.

The Factors and Discounters Association is the professional body for this type of finance. Their website at www.factors.org.uk is a good starting point.

Costs and benefits

The basic cost element is the finance charge. This is usually a percentage charge tied to the base rate. A typical charge would be 3% over base rate, but this may be negotiated. Typically, the rate is higher for factoring because the businesses are usually smaller and perceived as higher risk.

The second element of the charge is the administration fee. Because factoring involves administration of the sales ledger, this fee will be higher. Factoring can be helpful to smaller businesses as it frees up management time for more creative and strategic matters.

Benefits
- The main benefit is the immediate cash injection.

- In addition, growing businesses will receive increasing finance as the value of the debtors in their sales ledger increases.

- This finance facility grows with the business.

- There is no restriction on the way the cash generated in this manner can be used.

Disadvantages
- Apart from the cost, the major concern of client businesses is the loss of control.

- Smaller businesses fear that the finance company may adopt a tougher stance on chasing slow-paying customers, with the attendant risk of losing those customers.

- A similar concern is that the finance company will impose lower credit limits on customers' accounts, particularly with non-recourse finance.

- The finance company accepting bad debt risk will enforce credit controls, including setting lower credit limits, much more tightly than one with a recourse agreement.

◆ External misconception is also sometimes considered a drawback. A possible perception of factoring and disclosed invoice discounting finance is that it is a source of 'last resort' finance. The business using this type of finance may therefore be suspected of being in financial difficulties. However, this misconception was commoner in the earlier days and is fast disappearing.

Bills of exchange

A bill of exchange is a written agreement requiring the person to whom it is addressed to pay a specified sum at a future specified date. Customers sometimes use this form of finance to pay a supplier. The supplier may keep the bill of exchange until it matures or discount it. Discounting consists of accepting payment of the amount of the bill, less a discount factor. An institution such as a bank is the discounter, and that institution keeps the bill until it matures then presents it to the payer.

This method is not commonly used within the UK presently, but is more widespread in overseas trading.

FINANCE LEASES AND HIRE PURCHASE

These are alternative methods of financing the purchase of an asset. Although the substance of the transaction is the same, the form is different. Under these schemes, the legal ownership of the asset remains with the finance company, and under the contract the borrower is only actually hiring or leasing the asset until it is paid for.

We saw in Chapter 3 that one of the fundamental principles of financial reporting is 'substance over form'.

Thus the substance of the transaction of a finance lease is that the buyer is obtaining finance to buy the asset. Therefore this must be reflected in the financial statements by showing the asset in the balance sheet and the borrowing as a liability.

In contrast, the substance of an 'operating lease' is that the lessor actually retains long-term ownership of the asset (usually land or property) and the lessee pays a periodic charge for the temporary use of it. This is shown in the financial statements of the company by a rent or leasing charge as a deduction from profits, as part of the overheads or direct costs.

Finance leases are a popular way of raising finance for specific assets, for several reasons:

- They are flexible. Cancellation clauses can provide for updating the equipment concerned where technology and change are important factors.

- The finance cost is often reasonable because the asset itself is the security for the loan.

- The cash outflow is spread over the life of the asset.

- Lease finance can be obtained more readily than with other forms of finance – partly because it is usually for lower amounts, and partly because the security means that the leasing company does not have to require such stringent credit checks as other forms of lending.

Sale and leaseback

This involves selling an asset to a finance company and at the same time entering into an agreement to lease the asset back under an operating lease. This is often done with freehold property since it can release a large amount of cash. As the arrangement is an operating lease, all payments under it will be tax deductible.

Disadvantages of this include the fact that a liability to capital gains tax may arise on the sale of the asset. More significantly, the company has given up any future appreciation in the capital value of the asset.

11

Equity Capital

Share capital is the backbone of any company's finance. In this chapter we look at the types of equity capital sources for a company and dividend policy. We also look at issues of retaining control in private companies and repaying capital to shareholders.

SHARE CAPITAL

The ordinary shares represent the investments of people who are willing to take commercial risks. The liability of shareholders for company debts is limited to the amount they have invested in the company. Historically, limited liability provided the boost needed for investment in businesses, and provided the growth potential for the Industrial Revolution.

Ordinary shares

The ordinary share capital of a company is its financial lifeblood.

Ordinary shareholders form the bulk of the membership of the company, and they control the company by their votes. The management of the company is delegated to directors who are answerable to the shareholders.
Ordinary shareholders can only receive dividends out of any profits left after the prior claims of other investors,

including loan creditors and preference shareholders.

Preference shares

> As the name suggests, preference shares have a prior claim on the profits and assets of the company.

Preference shares rank before ordinary shares in paying dividends and in the distribution of assets in the case of the winding up of the company.

They therefore present a lower-risk profile and the returns are correspondingly lower. Typically, preference shares carry the right to a fixed dividend, which is usually cumulative. Thus, if the company was unable to pay the preference dividend in any year, it is rolled over to the following year.

There are different types of preference shares:

- *Participating preference shares.* These shares give preference shareholders the right to participate in the variable dividend paid to ordinary shareholders after their fixed dividend has been paid.

- *Redeemable preference shares.* These shares have a fixed repayment date. Because of this factor, they are seen as a lower risk investment and therefore carry a lower rate of fixed dividend.

- *Convertible preference shares.* These shares carry the

right to convert into ordinary shares at a fixed price at specified future dates. They work in a similar way to the convertible loan stocks seen in the previous chapter.

Deferred shares

Some companies issue deferred shares, which rank after ordinary shares in the 'pecking order'. Because of this, the risk profile is higher and investors in deferred shares would expect a greater reward.

CAPITAL MARKETS

To be able to raise money from the general public, a company must be a public limited company (plc) rather than a private company (ltd). However, there must also be a mechanism to enable the company to raise the new capital it needs, and for shareholders to sell or buy shares. In this section we will look at these markets and consider the efficiency of capital markets in fulfilling this function.

In the UK, the markets that exist to fulfil this requirement are the London Stock Exchange, the Alternative Investments Market (AIM) and the Unlisted Securities Market (USM). We look at the London Stock Exchange, although similar principles apply to the other two markets. Its functions are:

1. To provide a *primary* market for companies to raise new capital. Companies use the market to make new

share issues (see further details below) or issues of new debenture or loan stocks.

2. To provide a *secondary* market for investors to buy or sell their shares to other investors. If investors are assured of a market to sell their shares or buy extra ones, they are more likely to invest in a company.

A company must meet fairly stringent requirements relating to the size of the company, its past profit history, disclosure of information and so on for its shares to be traded on the Stock Exchange. In addition, there are requirements to issue regular information, the disclosure requirements being stricter than those of the Companies Act and Accounting Standards.

Once a company is listed, analysts employed by stockbrokers and financial journalists will closely monitor its activities.

The degree of scrutiny it suffers may not always be welcome but is an inevitable consequence of a listing.

ISSUING SHARES

A company may raise equity capital in different ways, depending on whether it is a public company or a private company. A private company may raise equity capital by the participators in the company – often a small number of people, perhaps members of the same family – buying shares privately. Public companies have ways to make public offers (see below).

Issue price and share premiums

Shares are designated by their class and their nominal value (for example, 'Ordinary shares of 25p'), and may be issued at the nominal value.

However, shares may be issued at a premium. That is to say, the shareholder pays more than the nominal value of the shares. The company must account for this premium, and hold it in a special account which may only be used for certain restricted purposes.

A public company may make a public offer of its shares.

Public offers

The mechanism is that the company makes an offer of sale of its shares by advertisement in newspapers and the publication of a prospectus. This sets out details of the shares on offer and various other relevant details of the company's finances, including, crucially, the reason for the issue of shares to raise money. The company itself sets the price, and takes the risks of the issue.

Underwriting

In making an issue of shares, a company will often have the issue underwritten, to minimise the risk.

This means that an exterior organisation, either stockbrokers or merchant bankers, act as the 'issuing house', which publishes the prospectus and arranges for institutional investors, such as pension funds or insurance companies, to guarantee to buy any shares not taken up by the general public or the existing shareholders. This incurs a fee, payable to the underwriting institution. In practice, the institution passes on a proportion of this fee to the institutional or private investors who have agreed to take the risk of buying the shares.

Issue by tender

This is another way of making a public issue of shares. The public is invited to make bids to offer to buy a specified number of shares at a price they offer. When the deadline for bids has passed, the company works out the right price, known as the striking price, to raise the money it requires from all the bids received, taking into account the quantities and prices bid for. All offers received below the striking price will be rejected, and all offers at or above the striking price accepted at the striking price.

Rights and scrip issues

Rights issues

Rights issues are made to raise additional capital, as described in Appendix 2. This method provides a relatively cheap way for a company to raise more equity capital. The risk is less than in making a public issue because the existing shareholders are more likely to take up the rights issue offer. The rights certificate may be sold, and the value of this can be calculated by reference to the existing share price and the offer price of the new shares.

There is a risk involved in making a rights issue, however. The risk is based on the fact that, for a rights issue to be successful, the offer price cannot be higher than the currently quoted share price. Otherwise, the shareholder would have no incentive to take up the rights issue. The company therefore has to make the offer sufficiently attractive by offering the shares at a discount. The risk is that during the inevitable time gap between the offer price being decided and the final date for acceptance of the offer, the share price might have fallen below the offer price.

Scrip issues

Scrip issues (also known as bonus issues), consist of an issue of free new shares to existing shareholders, and are often useful in expanding companies when the company wishes to make its shares more marketable.

> A scrip issue simply increases the number of shares in issue so the market price will fall correspondingly.

Thus, if the scrip issue was 1 for 1, the number of shares in issue will double and the price would be expected to halve. However, the reason for the issue is often that the share price is becoming too highly priced. Thus, for example one share priced at £10 is harder to sell than two shares priced at £5 each. Therefore, although in theory the market capitalisation should not change, the company's shares often become more marketable.

However, it often happens that scrip issues are made by expanding companies and are accompanied by dividend increases. The share price after a scrip issue therefore often performs better than before.

From the company's viewpoint, making a scrip issue transfers money out of reserves into the paid-up share capital of the company. This means that reserves that were previously distributable are now not distributable. Although this may not seem to be a positive signal, in fact it tends to generate confidence among potential investors, and lenders see this as a boost to the confidence in the company, because the larger the equity base of the company, the less risk exposure there is to lenders.

CLASSES OF SHARES AND RETAINING CONTROL

We have touched on the difference between private and public companies. As long as a company remains a private company, the owners of the shares (often members of a family) can exercise effective control. Once it 'goes public', however, that control is diluted or lost. In between there is often a stage where the original owners wish to retain control but need to raise more capital than they can afford privately.

Issuing different classes of shares can often accomplish this. Restricted or non-voting shares can be issued. Thus there could be 'A' shares, 'B' shares, and so on, with theoretically no limit to the number of classes of shares.

This way, dividends can be declared at different rates for each class of share. This method is often used when a patriarchal figure who started a company wishes his children to take over the company. He can issue different classes of shares to his children with restricted voting rights in order to retain control of the decisions and choose what dividends to pay on each class of shares. When he judges the time is right, he can sell some of his shares to his children to give them some of the control and voting rights.

REPAYING CAPITAL TO SHAREHOLDERS

There may be occasions when a company has surplus cash it wishes to return to its shareholders.

There are several ways of doing this.

1. Buying its own shares on the stock market. This involves paying the going rate for the shares.

2. Buying shares from its shareholders by private agreement. This can involve repurchasing the shares from the shareholders as a whole, or from certain classes or groups.

3. Making a tender offer to all shareholders. This involves offering to buy the shares at a specified price within a certain period.

Repurchasing shares involves their cancellation after they have been repurchased.

Special dividends
An alternative method of returning cash to shareholders is by way of a special dividend.

VENTURE CAPITAL
This form of finance consists of funding provided by a bank or other institutional investor in return for a stake in

the business. In this way, they become a partner in the business, taking risks and reaping rewards. The venture capitalist does not usually take an active part in managing the business, although they can often provide advice through long experience of this sort of financing. They also often provide valuable contacts and inside knowledge.

Who are venture capitalists?

The main providers of venture capital in the UK are firms funded by institutions such as pension funds, insurance companies or banks. They invest primarily in private or unquoted companies. The British Venture Capitalist Association represents the vast majority of the firms in this field.

Types of venture capital

Venture capitalists identify different stages of business development for which they would be prepared to consider providing finance. Because of the differing needs of each stage, their approach varies according to the stage. The stages of business life and the varying types of finance required were seen in Chapter 8.

Criteria

Venture capitalists put significant amounts of money into what could potentially be a business risk.

They therefore wish to satisfy themselves of several things before they invest their money.

- *Market potential.* The potential of the project for which capital is required will be investigated thoroughly. If there is no prospect of the project becoming a commercial success, they will not risk their money. If they see the opportunity to create a new market by an innovative new product or service, they are more likely to support that than a project which aims at penetrating an existing market against competitors.

- *Management.* Venture capitalists will assess the management team, its experience and skills. They must decide whether they think the management can carry through the project to achieve the objective.

The business seeking venture capital must make a strong, convincing case, with business plans, for the project. We saw in Chapter 9 the contents of a business plan, and the following essential elements should be covered:

- the ideals and strategy of the business;

- the management skills and experience of the personnel involved;

- the management structure and how the project may modify this;

- the market in which the business operates, with strengths and weaknesses of the competitors;

- the commercial viability of the product or service, with market research details;

- the prospects for growth of demand for the product or service;

♦ the nature and amount of the funding required.

Venture capitalists' involvement

Once the money has been invested, the venture capitalist will monitor the business regularly but not become involved in the day-to-day management. Their involvement means that management will be much more answerable to them. Besides sharing in profits, the venture capitalist will be more interested in the methods and accountability of the management team.

The business obtaining venture capital must submit regular management accounts to the venture capitalist and be subject to monitoring visits. This involvement should not be seen as a disadvantage. The venture capitalist, in seeking to protect his investment, will also be working for the benefit of the business and any advice should be viewed in a constructive light.

Incentives

There are certain tax incentives to venture capital. These are detailed in my book *Small Business Tax Guide* (How To Books, 2003).

DIVIDEND POLICY

Equity capital has a cost, and this cost is the dividends paid on the shares.

However, dividends do not generally distribute the whole of the profit. Management must decide a policy on dividend distribution.

The dividend policy pursued by a company can have a

radical effect on the value of shares, whether the company is quoted on the Stock Exchange or not. This at least is the traditional view, but it has been challenged in academic circles. The evidence is that managers of companies *perceive* that a company's dividend policy is important in improving the wealth of shareholders.

The nature of dividends

Dividends represent the return on shareholders' investment in the company's business. As such, shareholders expect a reward for taking risks.

Company law imposes limits on the amount of money that can be distributed as dividends.

◆ *Private companies* may only distribute *realised* profits.

◆ *Public companies* may distribute profits, whether they have been realised or not. However, these profits must be calculated in accordance with generally accepted accounting principles.

Dividend cover

Let us recap on the subject of dividend cover. This term refers to the difference between the amount of profits made and the amount distributed as dividends. The 'cover' is expressed as a multiple of the dividends distributed.

You should strive to maintain a good level of dividend cover – that is, you should not distribute all of your profit.

There are two main reasons why this is considered prudent practice.

◆ Retaining profits, or 'ploughing the profits back' into the business, is a good source of internal finance.

◆ A good level of dividend cover means that dividends are not liable to fluctuate severely, particularly when profits vary.

Example 11.1 shows how the level of dividend cover affects the ability of companies to continue to pay dividends.

Example 11.1

Two companies, ABC Ltd and XYZ Ltd, both make a profit in their first year of £500,000. They both have issued share capital of £1 million. Company ABC Ltd declares a dividend of 50p per share, and company XYZ Ltd declares a dividend of 20p per share.

The following year, they both make profits of £350,000. What will be the effect of this on the ability to pay dividends?

Company ABC Ltd distributed all of its profits in the first year. This means that the dividend was covered once. Company XYZ's dividend was covered 2.5 times.

In the second year, company ABC Ltd does not have any accumulated profits brought forward because it has paid them all out in the first year. Therefore it can only declare a maximum dividend of 35p on its shares for the second year, which is less than the first year's dividend.

Company XYZ Ltd retained £300,000 of its profits from the first year, and with the profits from the second year it now has £650,000 accumulated profits in the second year. It could, in

▶

theory, declare a dividend of up to 65p per share. In practice it can easily maintain its dividend of 20p per share, even increase it, and still have profits retained in the business.

The form of dividends

The usual expectation is that dividends will be distributed in the form of cash. In theory, however, they could be distributed in any form. A chain of supermarkets, for example, could distribute profits in the form of groceries to its shareholders. However, this would be impracticable.

Sometimes, however, profits are distributed in a different form to cash. The most common form of alternative payment is extra shares in the company, known as a scrip dividend.

Appendix 1

Self-diagnosis Credit Control Health Check and Ten Danger Signals to Look Out For

Below is a self-diagnosis health check. Take a few minutes to work through this and see how your business measures up. Answer the questions honestly to help identify the areas where weaknesses can be put right.

Self-diagnosis health check	Always	Usually	Sometimes	Never
Monitoring debtors				
Do you regularly use ratio analysis and calculate total debtor days of sales?				
Do you know which are your valuable customers?				
Credit checks				
Do you do a credit check on all new customers?				
Does your credit check include at least one request for a reference?				
Do you regularly renew credit checks on your main customers?				
Terms				
Do you agree written terms of business with all customers?				
Do your terms of business include payment terms?				
Do you require cash with order or deposits from customers with unsatisfactory credit checks?				
Do you set credit limits for all customers?				
Do the customers know their credit limits?				

Self-diagnosis health check	Always	Usually	Sometimes	Never
Invoicing				
Do you check the accuracy of all invoices — as to quantities, prices, calculations, delivery, etc.?				
Do you send invoices immediately on despatch of goods or completion of services?				
Do your invoices include payment terms and due date for payment?				
Do you reference your invoices to the customer's order?				
Do you confirm receipt of invoice and goods for large amounts?				
Monthly procedures				
Do you produce an aged debtors list?				
Do you send statements to each customer with transactions or a balance owing each month?				
Do you send appropriate chasing letters?				
General				
Do you know for each customer who is the best contact person for the sales ledger?				
Do you offer discounts or other incentives for prompt payment?				
Do you resolve customers' complaints immediately?				
Collection				
Do you charge interest on long overdue accounts?				
Do you know when each debt is due for payment?				
Do you phone major debtors before payment date to ensure that payment is authorised and that there are no complaints?				
Do you chase outstanding debts a week after they are overdue?				
Do you prioritise your collection to chase largest amounts first?				
Do you stop further supplies to customers who are long overdue?				
Do you use outside collection agencies if necessary?				

Self-diagnosis health check	Always	Usually	Sometimes	Never
Do you use the small claims court procedure where appropriate?				
Management procedures				
Do you have written procedures and timescales for handling and resolving complaints?				
Do you have a monthly review of problem accounts to agree courses of action?				
Do you have an easily understandable system of measuring the success of your credit control?				

For the above 32 questions, score 5 for each tick in the left-hand column, then 3, 2 and 1 for each succeeding column. If you scored over 140, you will probably not find much difficulty in realising the money tied up in debtors. For any score below 100, you probably need to make a comprehensive overhaul of your systems. Whatever your score, look carefully at the areas of low scores and try to improve on those areas.

DANGER SIGNALS TO LOOK OUT FOR

Here are ten scenarios which are typical of businesses with a poor credit control. Do you recognise any of them? If so, take action now.

◆ The terms of business have not been agreed.

◆ The payment terms have not been agreed. You just assume that everybody works on a '30 days' credit' cycle. The customer thinks that 60 days is acceptable.

◆ Your salesperson has made an unauthorised agreement to accept later payment in order to make the sale.

- The customer's buyer agrees to a 30-day payment, but the customer's bought ledger department works on a 60-day cycle.

- The customer's queries have not been dealt with. Your credit control department treats the debt as overdue but the customer treats it as under query.

- Hardened customers have learned just how far they can push your credit.

- You do not want to 'upset' the customer by asking for payment.

- You are not consistent in applying credit control procedures.

- Your credit control procedures have inbuilt delays.

- If your computer breaks down, you have no way of knowing how much customers owe you.

If you recognise over five of these as applying to you, your credit control system needs a thorough overhaul. Any one of these must be put right without delay.

Appendix 2

Investment Terms

CLASSES OF SHARES

The share capital of a company may not consist entirely of ordinary shares. Different classes of shares may exist, giving different rights to their holders. In theory, there could be an infinite number of different types of shares. However, the following are the most common:

Ordinary shares

These give the shareholders the right to participate in the profits of the company by way of a variable dividend declared from time to time. Ordinary shares usually carry the greatest degree of risk and are compensated by the greatest degree of reward in the company's profits.

Preference shares

These shares have preference in the event of the liquidation of a company. However, the reward is potentially not so great as for ordinary shares. It is usually a fixed rate, expressed as a percentage. The preference dividend is paid before any dividend on the ordinary shares. The interest rate paid on these shares is, however, still a dividend. That means that it is dependent on the company making a profit. In contrast, loan capital does not confer ownership of the company, and the interest is a charge on the profits of the company, paid whether or not the company makes a profit.

However, most preference shares are cumulative in nature. Therefore, if the company cannot pay a preference dividend one year, that means that there is also no dividend on the ordinary shares. However, if sufficient profit is made the following year, the arrears of the preference dividend are made up as well as paying the current preference dividend.

Convertible preference shares

Preference shares may be convertible. This means that they may be converted into ordinary shares at specified dates and for a predetermined price. Investors look to this form of share for a relatively high dividend yield with good prospects of capital growth.

Deferred shares

Occasionally a company may issue deferred shares, which have rights deferred below those of ordinary shares.

Redeemable shares

Shares of any class may be redeemable. This means that the company has the right to buy back those shares at specified dates, and at a price either predetermined or the method of calculation of which is predetermined. The memorandum and articles of the company must have special provisions allowing the company to redeem its shares. Unless specifically stated, shares are not redeemable.

Nominal value of shares

All shares have a nominal value. This is the nominal amount which each share contributes to the capital of the company. Thus, shares described as ordinary shares of £1 each have a nominal value of £1. The original issue of the shares by the company is usually for this nominal amount. However, shares may often be issued by the company at a premium.

Just as the nominal value of a share is not necessarily the amount paid for it, it is also not necessarily the amount which would be received if the company wound up. In the event of a winding up of a company, there is a definite order in which various creditors of the company are paid out. All creditors must be paid out before the shareholders (i.e. the owners of the company) can be paid anything. Then, if there are any preference shares, they are paid out before any ordinary shares. Thus ordinary shares rank last in the queue (unless there are deferred shares). If there is insufficient money left, ordinary shareholders could get back less than the nominal value of the shares.

By the same token, however, if there were more money left over after all others were paid off, the ordinary shareholders would get back more than the nominal value of the shares.

Warrants

Warrants give their owner the right to buy a certain quantity of shares in the company at a fixed price at some future date. The warrants themselves can be bought and sold. If they confer the right to buy the shares at a significantly lower price than the market price, then they are obviously valuable, and the price of the warrants would be roughly equivalent to the discount which the warrants represent.

Warrants are generally issued by companies to share-holders in proportion to the number of shares currently held. Because they are treated differently for tax purposes they can be more valuable to shareholders, and therefore can be seen as of greater value than a straightforward dividend. For the company they can be a way of raising additional capital.

Rights issue

This is a way for a company to raise more equity capital. Existing shareholders are given the right to buy additional shares in the company at a specified price. This price is usually at a discount to the current market price of the shares. If the shareholder does not wish to or have the money to take up the rights – i.e. to buy the new shares – the rights certificate may be sold.

Rights issues are generally expressed in terms of the proportion of new shares offered to existing shareholders and in terms of the price at which the new shares may be bought. For example, a rights issue could be 1 new share for every 4 existing shares at a price of 80p per share.

Scrip issue (or bonus issue)

This is an issue of free new shares by a company, expressed in terms of the proportion of new shares issued to the existing holding. Thus a scrip issue could be, say, 3 new shares for every 10 existing shares.

Debenture stocks

A debenture is a loan secured on particular assets of the company issuing it. It is usually redeemable at a specified future date, and bears a fixed rate of interest. Because it is secured on specific assets, there is greater security, and the risk is not so high. The yield on debentures would therefore not be expected to be as great as for unsecured borrowing.

Unsecured loans

Unsecured loans obviously do not have as much security as a debenture. They usually carry a fixed interest rate and a specified redemption date. However, because of their slightly higher risk factor, they would be expected to yield slightly higher than a debenture.

Floating rate loans

These loans can have the same characteristics as debentures or unsecured loans, but the one difference is that the interest rate is not fixed. It is a variable rate which moves in accordance with market rates of interest.

Convertible loans

These loans carry the option to convert the loans into ordinary shares of the company at specified dates and at a predetermined price. To this extent they are similar to convertible preference shares.

Market sector

In share price listings in newspapers, the companies are divided into different sectors. These represent the type of business carried on by the companies. Thus typical headings might include banks, electricity, real estate, pharmaceuticals, etc.

This classification enables investors and analysts to compare like with like when making a judgement about a company.

Market capitalisation

This is the measure of the size of the capital invested in the company. It consists of the total number of shares issued by the company multiplied by the share price.

Example

XYZ plc has 10 million shares in issue. The market price of the shares is £5 per share. Therefore the market capitalisation of the company is £50,000,000.

Since the price of the shares can fluctuate from day to day – even from hour to hour – the market capitalisation of the company fluctuates in the same way.

Earnings per share

This is a measure of the profits of the company attributable to each share. The formula is the net after tax profit divided by the number of shares in issue.

Example

The after-tax profit of XYZ plc for the year ended 31 December 2003 is £5 million. The company has 10 million shares in issue, so the earnings per share are £0.50.

This measure is invariably judged by the trend over a number of years. The increase or decline in earnings per share will be used by investors to make a judgement on the value of the shares.

Earnings growth

This is a simple measure of how the company's performance has improved or otherwise over the recent past. If a company is able to produce regular, even if unspectacular, earnings growth year after year, it is a good prospect for investors. If there is a dip in one year only, there may well be a valid reason. Investors will, however, not be keen to invest in a company of which the earnings per share regularly decrease.

Price-earnings ratio

This is the relationship between the price of a share and the earnings of the company. The measure is the number of times the earnings per share must be multiplied to arrive at the share price.

Example

The earnings per share of XYZ plc are £0.50. The share price is £5. Therefore, the price-earnings ratio is 10. The share price presents ten years' earnings.

This ratio can be compared with the market as a whole or with other companies in the same industry sector.

Quality of earnings

The price-earnings ratio described above is based on historic figures. For an investor, this information is not so relevant as future figures. However, historic figures are a known quantity, but future earnings are unknown and uncertain.

The price-earnings ratio when based on future forecasts is known as the prospective price-earnings ratio. The quality of earnings is based largely on 'market sentiment'. This stands for what stockbrokers' analysts think of the company and its future prospects. If they have doubts about the company, and in particular its ability to maintain the profit levels, then the quality of earnings is said to be low.

Dividend yield

The dividend paid by a company is expressed as an amount per share. To arrive at the dividend yield, the amount of the dividend is expressed as a percentage of the share price.

> *Example*
>
> The dividend for the year ended 31 December 2003 paid by XYZ plc is 20p per share. The market price of the shares is £5 per share, so the dividend yield is 4%.

The yield is calculated on the market price of the shares, not the nominal value of the shares. For example, if the nominal value of the shares is £1, the yield of the 20p dividend would appear to be 20%. However, the market price gives a truer reflection of the value of the shares and therefore of the real yield.

Dividend cover

This measure relates to the amount of 'cover' given to the dividends by the earnings of the company.

> **Example**
>
> The earnings of XYZ plc for the year ended 31 December 2003 are 50p per share. The dividend declared is 20p per share. The dividend cover is therefore 2.5 times.

The lower the dividend cover, the more vulnerable the dividends would be. If the company's profit decreased, there would be more chance of it not being able to pay a dividend in future.

Interest yield

This is a measure of the actual interest rate an investor would achieve on fixed interest stocks and bonds, including government stocks. It is calculated in a similar way to the dividend yield.

> **Example**
>
> XYZ plc has a loan (or debenture) stock. The nominal rate of interest is 12%, but the price of the stock is £150 for every £100 of nominal stock. Thus by simple division of the interest rate by the price the interest yield is seen to be 8%.

Interest yields are affected by the prevailing rates of interest and by the standing of the company which issued the stock or bond. Thus loan stocks or bonds issued by 'blue chip' companies are said to be 'investment grade' issues. The yield on these is less than the yield on lower grade issues, i.e. those issued by companies with a slightly lower reputation. The increased yield on lower grade bonds is a reflection of the increased risk attaching to these issues.

Redemption yield

This term relates to the comparison of yields from fixed-interest stocks or bonds, including government stocks. The comparison goes one step further than the interest yield calculation. It does this by taking into account the premium or discount in the price of the stock or bond. In effect, what it measures is the total return on the investment if it were held until the redemption date.

Example

The XYZ plc stock referred to in the example above shows an interest yield of 8%. However, the redemption yield would be quite different if the stock had, say, six years to redemption compared with 20 years to redemption. The redemption yield with six years to redemption would be 2.4%, but the redemption yield with 20 years to redemption would be 6.3%.

The redemption yield calculation gives a truer comparison of the real yield on interest-bearing stocks or bonds.

Net asset value

This is the total assets of the company less all of the liabilities – be they short-term liabilities, long-term liabilities, provisions for losses, etc.

Net asset value per share

This is the net asset value of the company divided by the number of ordinary shares in issue. This gives a theoretical value of the assets represented by each share. The comparison of this value with the share price gives a discount or premium. This measure is particularly important in property companies and investment trust companies.

Appendix 3

Useful Websites

Below are some helpful websites.

GOVERNMENT BODIES

Business Link   www.businesslink.org

This is an official government body, but the website is packed full of useful tips, information, links and advice. One of the most useful of all government sites for the self-employed.

Companies House   www.companies-house.gov.uk

This is the central registration agency for all limited companies.

Customs and Excise   www.hmce.gov.uk

This is the site of Customs and Excise, which administers VAT. A whole section of the site is devoted to VAT matters.

Department of Trade and Industry   www.dti.gov.uk

This is the government department dealing with all matters relating to trade and industry.

Department of Work and Pensions   www.dwp.gov.uk

This is the name of the new department, since June 2001, dealing with work, family and pensions. Social Security contributions are now dealt with by the Inland Revenue.

Inland Revenue   www.inlandrevenue.gov.uk

This site is very useful, and gives a lot of helpful advice for the self-employed, as well as general tax advice.

Insolvency Service www.insolvency.gov.uk
Easy-to-use site from the government's official insolvency service.

Office of Fair Trading www.oft.gov.uk
This is the site of the Office of Fair Trading, dealing with all aspects of consumer regulation and law. Its slogan is 'Protecting customers; encouraging competition'.

Serious Fraud Office www.sfo.gov.uk
The Serious Fraud Office is the government body dealing with fraud and has links to international fraud prevention organisations.

OTHER OFFICIAL AND SEMI-OFFICIAL BODIES

Advertising Standards Authority www.asa.org.uk
This body is the watchdog for advertising complaints.

Association of British Insurers www.abi.org
This is the body representing British insurance companies.

Association of Chartered Certified Accountants
www.acca.co.uk
This is the site of the body governing certified accountants, and can put you in touch with them.

British Bankers' Association www.bba.org.uk
This site provides information which will help you understand the various banking considerations a business might encounter at various stages of its business cycle.

British Chambers of Commerce
www.britishchambers.org.uk
This body coordinates the work of the many local chambers of

commerce and trade, which bring together businesses in local areas, to represent them in matters of local importance – such as rating problems and fighting business crime.

British Franchise Association   www.british-franchise.org.uk
This is the body for franchising operations of all sorts.

British Venture Capitalist Association   www.bvca.co.uk
This is the national body representing venture capitalists.

Factors and Discounters Association   www.factors.org.uk
This is the body for factoring and invoice discounting finance companies.

Federation of Small Businesses   www.fsb.org.uk
This independent body champions the cause of small businesses. It is the UK's largest small business lobby group. The site gives advice and help on all sorts of matters, including things like dealing with late payers.

Institutes of Chartered Accountants
                              www.chartered-accountants.co.uk
This site covers the Institutes in England and Wales, Scotland, and Ireland. It can put you in touch with chartered accountants anywhere in these regions.

National Federation of Enterprise Agencies   www.nfea.com
This is the national organisation of Enterprise Agencies.

Telework Association   www.tca.org.uk
This is Europe's largest network association for teleworkers. The website gives information about all aspects of teleworking, including items about telecottages.

BANKS

Alliance and Leicester   www.alliance-businessbanking.co.uk

This is the business banking site of Alliance and Leicester. This also covers the Girobank, which manages a large proportion of the cash handled by businesses in the UK.

Barclays Bank   www.barclays.co.uk/business

Barclays bank has a dedicated section of its website for business banking.

BUSINESS ANGELS, MENTORS AND INCUBATORS

Angel Bourse   www.angelbourse.com

Business Incubator Network   www.ukbi.co.uk

An sssociation of 'incubators' giving mentoring and other help to new businesses.

London Business Angels   www.businessangels-london.co.uk

A source for business angels in the London area.

National Business Angels Network   www.nban.com

The national organisation for business angels.

The Venture Site Ltd   www.venturesite.co.uk

This site links businesses requiring capital with business angels wanting to invest.

CREDIT MANAGEMENT AND INSURANCE

Better Payment Practice Group   www.payontime.co.uk

This site provides free information and advice on credit management, including a 'business doctor'. This is an organisation set up by the British Chambers of Commerce to encourage businesses to pay debts on time and to advise businesses on better credit management practices.

Coverclick   www.coverclick.com

This firm provides credit insurance against insolvency of customers and late payment.

Creditcheckit   www.creditcheckit.co.uk

This company provides information about firms with whom you want to do business – such as the trading history, directors, finances, etc.

Credit To Cash   www.ctoc.co.uk

This site gives advice on cashflow management.

LloydsTSB Commercial Finance   www.ltsbcf.co.uk

This is the commercial finance arm of LloydsTSB, offering credit insurance against customer insolvency and late payment.

NCM Direct   www.ncm-direct.com

An insurance company providing credit insurance.

FIGHTING FRAUD

Control Risk Group   www.crg.com

This includes sections on IT security and investigation services.

Fraud Prevention   www.fraud.co.uk

This site gives information on fraud over a wide range of sectors including accounting, banking and insurance.

Kroll   www.krollworldwide.com

This site provides up-to-date business intelligence.

Public Concern at Work   www.pcaw.co.uk

This organisation is a registered charity aimed at 'making whistle-blowing work'.

Scambusters   www.scambusters.com

This site provides plenty of examples of Internet scams and the latest news.

US National Fraud Information Centre   **www.fraud.org**

This site provides information about the latest scams, particularly those on the Web.

INDEPENDENT COMMERCIAL ORGANISATIONS

Better Business   **www.better-business.co.uk**

This is the website of the business magazine of the same name. It gives information on many areas, including producing business plans.

Beyond Bricks   **www.beyondbricks.com**

This is part of the DTI's mentoring initiative. It is particularly slanted towards internet entrepreneurs.

Bizwise   **www.bizwise.co.uk**

This site offers a wide range of business advice, for a subscription – at the time of writing, £10 per month or £99 per year. You can also use this site to market your business on their register.

Business Finance   **www.businessfinance.uk.net**

Desk Demon   **www.DeskDemon.co.uk**

This site provides many free office tools, and a Royal Mail postcode search and telephone directory search.

Enterprise Advisory Service International

www.govgrants.com

This organisation provides a service to businesses searching for government grants. It operates on a commercial basis, charging a modest fee to members.

Exchange and Mart   **www.exchangeandmart.co.uk**

This is the famous source of second-hand goods. It has a business section for all kinds of business equipment and services.

Just for Business **www.j4b.co.uk**

This site gives access to a database of grants available to businesses. Registered users will also receive regular updates on new developments which may affect them.

Markets Unlocked **www.MarketsUnlocked.com**

This is a UK-based marketplace for buying and selling. It claims to deal with everything your company buys, everything your company sells, in every industry sector, in every country.

Marylebone Warwick Balfour **www.mwb.co.uk**

This company specialises in investment in the property sector, looking specifically at underdeveloped property. Sectors such as hotels, leisure parks and retail stores could find help here.

MTI **www.mtifirms.com**

This is a venture capital manager, providing funds in the form of equity capital to expanding businesses.

Pipex Websell **www.websell.pipex.net**

This company is a Payment Service Provider, which handles the requirements of accepting credit card and debit card transactions over the Internet.

SPSS **www.spss.com**

This company produces software packages of statistical techniques which can be used in financial management, among other areas. Their picturesque name for their product is 'data mining'.

Startups **www.startups.co.uk**

This site gives advice over a wide range of subjects, from starting up and franchising through to business structure, the law, business equipment, working at home and much more.

Virginbiz   **www.virginbiz.net**

Another good site with lots of advice. This one also pushes many of its own products.

WJB Chiltern   **www.wjbchiltern.com**

This firm provides advisory services to companies seeking to raise equity or develop business plans.

Working From Home   **www.wfh.co.uk**

This site is a British Telecom site for those working from home. It gives a link to other people working from home. It provides a forum, links to useful sites and business tips.

Glossary

Accounting conventions Conventions taken as normal in the drawing up of financial statements.

Asset turnover A measure of the usage of fixed assets in generating turnover.

Audit Independent examination of accounts.

Break even point The level of turnover at which the income and expenses will be equal.

Bill of exchange Instrument giving credit to purchaser of goods or services.

Budget Method of controlling costs and income by comparison with forecasts.

Business angels Individuals offering finance and assistance.

Cost accounting Methods of arriving at costs of items produced.

Credit control Control of monies owing from debtors.

Current assets Short-term assets which vary from day to day in the course of business.

Current liabilities Short-term liabilities.

Current ratio The relationship between current assets and current liabilities.

Discount Reduction in price given as incentive.

Discounted cash flow Method of appraising projects.

Equity The share capital of a company.

Factoring Method of raising finance on book debts.

Finance lease Means of financing the purchase of an asset.

Gearing The relationship between loan capital and share capital.

Hire purchase Means of financing the purchase of an asset.

Internal controls Systems of administrative checks on aspects of operations.

Internal rate of return Method of appraising projects.

Invoice discounting Method of raising finance on book debts.

Loan covenants Conditions in a loan agreement to ensure security for the lender.

Merger Combination of two similar sized businesses.

Organic growth Business growth from internal sources, not from acquisitions of other businesses.

Overdraft Arrangement with bank to permit the customer to draw in excess of the deposited funds.

Overtrading Lack of cash resources often encountered in growing businesses.

Project appraisal Methods of appraising the economic viability of future projects.

Quick ratio The relationship between all current assets except stock and work in progress to current liabilities.

Return on capital employed Profitability ratio showing the relationship between profit (before interest and taxation) and all long-term capital employed.

Rights issue Issue of shares to existing shareholders at preferential rates.

Scrip issue Issue of free shares to existing shareholders.

Sale and leaseback Method of fund raising by selling assets and then leasing them back.

Statistical analysis Method of using ratios between key figures in financial statements.

Stock turnover A measure of how quickly stock is used in the business.

SWOT analysis Analysis of strengths, weaknesses, opportunities and threats.

Takeover Acquisition of one business by another.

Term matching The process of matching finance provided with the object for which it is provided.

Treasury management The management of surplus cash resources.

Venture capital Equity finance offered by institutional investors.

Warrants Instruments giving the right to buy shares at a fixed price at a specified date.

Working capital Current assets less current liabilities.

Further Reading

Accounting and Finance for Managers J. Kind (Kogan Page)

The Art of Managing Finance D. Davies (McGraw Hill)

Business Finance E. McLaney (Financial Times/Prentice Hall)

Business Finance: Theory and Practice E. McLaney (Pitman)

Corporate Financial Management G. Arnold (Financial Times/ Pitman)

Credit Management R. Bass (Nelson Thornes)

The Finance Manual for Non-financial Managers P. Mckeon and L. Gough (Prentice Hall)

Financial Analysis B. Rees (Prentice Hall)

Financial Management and Decision Making J. Samuels et al (International Thomson Business Press)

The Financial Controls Handbook UK 200 Group – The Daily Telegraph

Financial Management for Non-Specialists P. Atrill (Financial Times/Prentice Hall)

Going for Self Employment J. Whiteley (How To Books)

Intermediate Financial Management E. Brigham et al (Thomson Learning)

Investment Appraisal and Financial Decisions S. Lumby and C. Jones (Chapman & Hall)

Management of Finance D. Cox and M. Fardon (Osborne Books)

Managing Financial Resources M. Broadbent and J. Cullen (Butterworth-Heinemann)

Mastering Financial Management J. Whiteley (Palgrave Macmillan)

Small Business Tax Guide J. Whiteley (How To Books)

Index